nitty gritty books

Seafoods Cookbook
Quick Breads
Pasta & Rice
Calorie Watchers Cookbook
Pies & Cakes
Yogurt
The Ground Beef Cookbook
Cocktails & Hors d'Oeuvres
Casseroles & Salads
Kid's Party Book
Pressure Cooking
Food Processor Cookbook
Peanuts & Popcorn
Kid's Pets Book
Make It Ahead French Cooking

Soups & Stews
Crepes & Omelets
Microwave Cooking
Vegetable Cookbook
Kid's Arts and Crafts
Bread Baking
The Crockery Pot Cookbook
Kid's Garden Book
Classic Greek Cooking
Low Carbohydrate Cookbook
Kid's Cookbook
Italian
Cheese Guide & Cookbook
Miller's German
Quiche & Souffle

To My Daughter, With Love
Natural Foods
Chinese Vegetarian
The Jewish Cookbook
Working Couples
Mexican
Sunday Breakfast
Fisherman's Wharf Cookbook
Barbecue Cookbook
Ice Cream Cookbook
Blender Cookbook
The Wok, a Chinese Cookbook
Japanese Country
Fondue Cookbook

designed with giving in mind

We dedicate this book to our husbands, Al and Chuck, and to our little muffins, John, Tami, David and Tom. We extend a special thank you to Jackie Walsh.

QUICK BREADS

by
Barbara Kanerva Kyte
Katherine Hayes Greenberg

Illustrated by Craig Torlucci

Edited by Maureen Reynolds

TABLE OF CONTENTS

INTRODUCTION

Remember the visits to Grandma's house and the tempting aromas drifting from her kitchen as she prepared mouth-watering, fresh-baked breads? Are those delicious goodies more than just memories of the past? Can you fit bread making into your busy life? Yes! Today you can recapture the joy of baking your own bread with a wide variety of quick bread recipes. Made without yeast, quick breads are fast, nutritious, and easy to prepare—and they taste just as yummy as the ones Grandma used to make!

Imagine starting your day with a basket of hot, tender biscuits served with a crock of butter and your favorite jam. For dinner, tempt your family with a generous square of corn bread topped with hot and hearty chili. Then satisfy your craving for a sweet treat by nibbling on honey nutbread. You'll find recipes for these and more. So why wait? Prepare your baking pans, preheat your oven and begin!

PREPARE YOUR PANTRY

You probably already have most of these basic ingredients in your pantry.

FLOUR, the major ingredient in quick breads, contains gluten, which gives the bread its structure. Wheat flours, such as whole wheat and unbleached all purpose flour, may be used separately or together to vary the texture of the bread. Whole wheat flour contains all of the wheat, including the bran and germ. It may be coarse or fine and should be stored in the refrigerator to protect the germ from turning rancid. Non-wheat flours, such as corn, oat, rye and soy, add variety to the taste and texture of quick breads and may be combined with wheat flours.

LIQUIDS, such as milk, fruit juice and water, dissolve the dry ingredients and hold the bread together.

LEAVENING AGENTS, such as baking powder, baking soda, eggs and steam, make the bread rise.

SHORTENINGS, such as butter, margarine and oils, add flavor and tenderness to the bread.

SWEETENERS, such as honey, sugar, molasses and maple syrup, add flavor and moisture to the bread. They also aid in browning. Breads made with liquid sweeteners are more moist and stay fresh longer.

EGGS give your bread rich flavor, texture and protein.

FLAVORINGS determine the character of the bread. By varying the flavorings, you can produce a whole variety of taste sensations from the same basic recipe. Flavorings include salt, extracts, herbs, spices, nuts, seeds, fruits and vegetables.

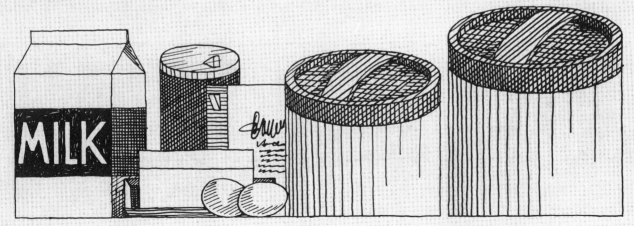

FOR GOOD MEASURE

Measuring ingredients accurately is an important step in making perfect quick breads. When measuring dry ingredients you do not need to sift. Sifting removes the bran and wheat germ particles from the whole wheat flour. Just spoon the flour, baking soda and baking powder into the measuring cup or spoon and level it off with the flat edge of a knife. When measuring liquids, pour them into a glass measuring cup and hold it at eye level to check for accuracy.

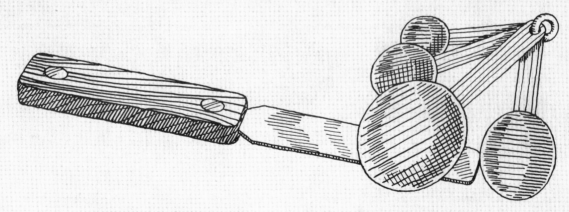

The following list of equivalents will help you with your shopping and measuring.

Apples, 1 lb.	equals	3 medium or 3 cups sliced or grated
Apricots, dried, 1 lb.	equals	3 cups dried or 5 cups cooked
Bananas, 1 lb.	equals	3 whole or 2-1/2 cups sliced, 1-1/2 cups mashed
Cheese, 1 lb.	equals	5 cups grated
Coconut, 1 lb.	equals	5 cups shredded
Dates, unpitted,1 lb.	equals	2-1/2 cups unpitted or 1-3/4 cups pitted
Lemon, 1 medium	equals	1 tbs. grated rind or 3 tbs. juice
Orange, 1 medium	equals	2 tbs. grated rind or 1/3 cup juice
Prunes, 1 lb.	equals	4-1/2 cups pitted and cooked
Raisins, 1 lb.	equals	3 cups

NATURAL SUBSTITUTIONS

Quick breads and natural ingredients are tasty and nutritious. You may wish to incorporate equal parts of whole wheat flour and unbleached flour into a recipe, instead of using all unbleached flour. Likewise, you may wish to substitute honey for sugar. If you do, be sure to compensate for this by decreasing the quantity of liquid in the recipe (see "Switching Your Sweeteners," below).

You may have a favorite quick bread recipe that calls for white flour and sugar. To substitute more nutritious ingredients, use the following guidelines:

FORTIFY YOUR FLOUR

Boost the nutrition of any quick bread recipe by including one tablespoon each of dried milk powder, wheat germ, and soy flour for every cup of flour.

One cup of white flour is equivalent to one cup of whole wheat flour. We like the ratio of half whole wheat flour and half all purpose flour. We have found that the texture this ratio produces is most pleasing to everyone. The more whole wheat flour you use, the heavier the texture will be.

SWITCHING YOUR SWEETENERS

One cup of sugar equals 3/4 cup of honey. To substitute honey for sugar, decrease the liquid in the recipe by 1/4 cup. If no liquid is specified, add four tablespoons of flour.

One cup of molasses equals one cup sugar. To substitute molasses for sugar, decrease the liquid in the recipe by 1/3 cup. Again, if no liquid is specified, add four tablespoons of flour.

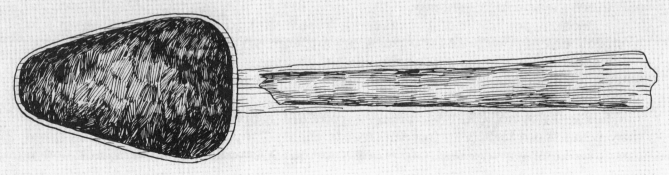

QUICK TIPS FOR BETTER QUICK BREADS

• Avoid the last minute rush at mealtime by mixing the dry ingredients several hours ahead of time, or the night before. It only takes a few minutes to add the liquid ingredients, bake and serve. If you are really on a tight schedule, you might find it convenient to keep a batch of Quick Mix on hand (see page 10).

• Unless otherwise specified, have all the ingredients in the recipe at room temperature. This will insure light and tender baked goods.

• Honey will slide right out of the measuring cup if you measure the oil in the recipe first. If no oil is called for in the recipe, coat the measuring cup lightly with oil before measuring the honey.

• Because you may not always have fresh buttermilk on hand, it is convenient to store a box of powdered buttermilk in your cupboard.

• Most quick breads are best when they are served right out of the oven. So, when they are finished baking, serve just enough to go around, and return the rest to the oven to keep warm.

• If you are not going to consume your quick breads within a few days, you may wrap them tightly in foil and freeze them. They may be frozen up to three months. When you are ready to enjoy your quick breads, thaw them, and warm

8

them in a 350°F. oven. It takes about five minutes to heat muffins and biscuits, and about ten minutes to heat loaves and coffee cakes.

- Day old muffins and biscuits are delicious when split, toasted and spread with butter.

- For quick and easy clean-up, use any of the following: teflon baking pans, paper liners for muffins, or disposalbe foil loaf pans.

QUICK MIX

For even quicker quick breads, try our Quick Mix for muffins, loaves, biscuits, coffee cakes, pancakes and waffles. You may adjust the proportions of whole wheat and unbleached all purpose flour to suit your taste.

Single Recipe
2/3 cup whole wheat flour
2/3 cup unbleached all purpose flour
1-1/2 tsp. baking powder
1/4 tsp. salt
1/4 cup butter **or** margarine

Quantity Recipe
3 cups whole wheat flour
3 cups unbleached all purpose flour
3 tbs. baking powder
1-1/2 tsp. salt
1 cup butter **or** margarine

Blend flour, baking powder and salt in mixing bowl. Using electric mixer, food processor or pastry blender, cut shortening into flour mixture until it resembles coarse cornmeal. Store tightly covered Quick Mix for up to two months in the refrigerator or up to four months in the freezer. A single recipe makes 2 cups of Quick Mix. A quantity recipe makes about 8 cups of Quick Mix.

BUTTERMILK QUICK MIX

For extra flavor and nutrition, add powdered buttermilk and baking soda to the dry ingredients in the above recipe.

Single Recipe
2 tbs. powdered buttermilk
1/8 tsp. baking soda

Quantity Recipe
1/2 cup powdered buttermilk
1/2 tsp. baking soda

When you see this symbol: ![symbol] you'll be able to tell at a glance, that the recipe beside it is especially easy because it uses Quick Mix.

DINNER MUFFINS
AND SWEET MUFFINS

Piping hot muffins are a special treat with meals or as snacks. Made with whole wheat flour, honey and other healthful ingredients, muffins are as nutritious as they are quick to prepare. Once you serve them to your family, they may become a tradition at your house.

The perfect muffin is moist, light and tender. Its texture is even and without tunnels. The top of the muffin is nicely rounded and golden brown. You may ask yourself, "How can I make these perfect muffins?" We have included a list of "secrets" we have accumulated over the years. They work for us, and we are sure that if you follow them, they will work for you!

• Most important of all: in the last step of the recipe, when you are instructed to combine the liquid and dry ingredients, **do not overmix!** Stir the two together only until the dry ingredients become moistened. Overmixing will cause tough muffins with tunnels.

• Because the final step is not a mixing process, but rather a combining process, it is important to have thoroughly stirred together the dry ingredients, and thoroughly beaten together the liquid ingredients, **before** the two are combined.

• When the dry ingredients have been well combined, form a "well" in the center of them. This will facilitate the "combining" process.

• Slowly add the honey to the other liquid ingredients in a fine stream. This will make blending a lot easier.

• After "combining" the liquid and dry ingredients, let the batter "rest" for a minute or two. This will give the leavening agents a chance to activate.

• Spoon the batter into greased or paper-lined muffin pans, filling them two-thirds full. For a special shape, try mini muffin pans, or bundt muffin pans. Remember, you must adjust the baking time according to the size and shape of the pans you use.

• Bake the muffins in a preheated oven. Test for doneness by gently pressing the center of a muffin. If it springs back, leaving little or no fingerprint, it is done. Or, you may insert a toothpick into a muffin, and if it comes out clean, the muffins are done.

• When you are keeping the muffins warm in the oven, tip each muffin on its side until you are ready for them. This will keep them moist.

QUICK PLAIN MUFFINS

So quick and easy to put together. Try some of our scrumptious variations on page 17.

1/2 cup milk
1 egg, well beaten
2 cups Quick Mix (see page 10)
1/4 cup sugar

Preheat oven to 400°F. Mix milk and egg together well. Add to Quick Mix and sugar. Stir until just moistened. Fill greased or paper lined muffin pans 2/3 full. Bake for 20 minutes, or until golden brown. Makes 10 muffins.

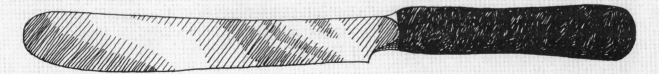

BASIC MUFFIN

Be creative with our variations!

3/4 cup whole wheat flour
1 cup unbleached all purpose flour } **or** 1-3/4 cups all purpose flour
2-1/2 tsp. baking powder
1/2 tsp. salt
1/2 cup milk when using honey (3/4 cup milk when using sugar)
1 egg, well beaten
1/3 cup oil
1/4 cup honey **or** sugar

Preheat oven to 400°F. Stir together flour, baking powder and salt. Mix milk, egg, oil and honey **or** sugar together well. Add this mixture to dry ingredients. Stir until just moistened. Fill greased or paper-lined muffin pans 2/3 full. Bake for 20 minutes, or until golden brown. Makes 12 muffins.

BASIC MUFFIN VARIATIONS

You may alter the "Basic Muffin" by adding one of the following to the dry ingredients:

- 3 tbs. fried bacon, crumbled
- 3 tbs. green onion, thinly sliced
- 1/4 tsp. dill, 1/2 tsp. oregano, and 1 tbs. snipped parsley
- 1/2 cup shredded cheddar cheese
- 1/2 cup shredded Swiss cheese, and 1 tsp. caraway seeds
- 1/4 cup powdered buttermilk and 1/2 tsp. baking soda
- 1/2 cup grated carrot
- 1/2 cup sunflower seeds

Also:
- Replace the milk with buttermilk and add 1/2 teaspoon of baking soda.
- Before baking, sprinkle the top of each muffin with about 1/4 teaspoon of paprika, Parmesan cheese or sesame seeds.

BRAN MUFFINS

These delicious muffins have an old-fashioned flavor. They taste just like the ones Grandma used to make!

1 cup whole wheat flour **or** all purpose flour
1 cup bran flakes
2-1/2 tsp. baking powder
1/2 tsp. baking soda
1/2 tsp. salt
1/2 cup raisins

1/4 cup sugar
1 egg, well beaten
2/3 cup buttermilk
1/4 cup oil
1/4 cup molasses

Preheat oven to 400°F. Stir together flour, bran, baking powder, baking soda, salt, raisins, and sugar. Mix egg, buttermilk, oil, and molasses together well. Add this mixture to dry ingredients. Stir until just moistened. Fill greased or paper-lined muffin pans 2/3 full. Bake for 20 minutes, or until done. Makes 12 muffins.

CORN MUFFINS

Serve piping hot with butter. In the South, honey is a must.

1/2 cup whole wheat flour
1/2 cup unbleached all purpose flour } **or** 1 cup all purpose flour
1 cup yellow cornmeal
1 tbs. baking powder
3/4 tsp. salt
1/4 cup sugar
1 cup milk
1 egg, well beaten
1/4 cup oil

Preheat oven to 400°F. Stir together flour, cornmeal, baking powder, salt and sugar. Mix milk, egg, and oil together well. Add this mixture to dry ingredients. Stir until just moistened. Let batter rest for five minutes. Fill greased or paper-lined muffin pans 2/3 full. Bake for 15 to 20 minutes, or until done. Makes 10 to 12 muffins.

VARIATIONS FOR CORN MUFFINS

Nine different muffins from one basic recipe!

Add one of the following to the dry ingredients:

- 1/4 cup fried bacon, crumbled
- 1/4 cup green onions, thinly sliced
- 3/4 tsp. dill
- 1/3 cup chopped tomato and 1 tsp. basil
- 1/2 cup grated cheese

- Fill muffin cups 1/2 full with batter. Drop 1/2 teaspoon of jam on each, then fill to 2/3 full with batter.
- Before baking, sprinkle the top of each muffin with about 1/4 teaspoon of Parmesan cheese or sesame seeds, **or** a dash of paprika.

GRANOLA MUFFINS

Use your favorite granola mix for this lunch box treat.

2 cups Quick Mix (see page 10)
1 cup granola
1 egg, well beaten
1 cup milk
2 tsp. cinnamon **or** nutmeg (optional)

Preheat oven to 400°F. Stir together Quick Mix and granola. Mix egg and milk together well. Add this mixture to dry ingredients. Stir until just moistened. Fill greased or paper-lined muffin pans 2/3 full. If desired, sprinkle batter lightly with cinnamon or nutmeg. Bake for 20 minutes, or until golden brown. Makes 12 muffins.

OATMEAL MUFFINS

Serve this muffin hot with butter and jam.

1 cup whole wheat flour **or** unbleached all purpose flour
1 cup Quick-cooking oatmeal
2-1/2 tsp. baking powder
1/2 tsp. baking soda
1/2 tsp. salt
1/4 cup brown sugar, firmly packed
1 egg, well beaten
3/4 cup buttermilk
1/3 cup oil

Preheat oven to 400°F. Stir together flour, oatmeal, baking powder, baking soda, salt and brown sugar. Mix egg, buttermilk and oil together well. Add this mixture to dry ingredients. Stir until just moistened. Fill greased or paper-lined muffin pans 2/3 full. Bake for 20 minutes, or until golden brown. Makes 12 muffins.

HOMESTEAD MUFFINS

Grandma's original recipe did not use salt. You may wish to add 1/2 teaspoon salt.

1 cup whole wheat flour
1 cup unbleached all purpose flour } **or** 2 cups all purpose flour
1 tbs. baking powder
1/2 tsp. salt (optional)
2 tbs. sugar
1 egg, well beaten
1 tbs. oil **or** melted butter **or** margarine
1 cup milk

Preheat the oven to 400°F. Stir the flour, baking powder, salt and sugar together. Mix the egg, oil and milk together well. Add this mixture to the dry ingredients. Stir until just moistened. Fill greased muffin pans 2/3 full. Bake for 20 minutes, or until golden brown. Makes 12 muffins.

SESAME WHEAT GERM MUFFINS

Try this super nutritious muffin!

1 cup whole wheat flour
3/4 cup wheat germ
2-1/2 tsp. baking powder
1/2 tsp. salt
1/4 cup sesame seeds
1 egg, well beaten
1/2 cup milk
1/4 cup oil
1/4 cup honey

Preheat the oven to 400°F. Stir together the flour, wheat germ, baking powder, salt and sesame seeds. Mix the egg, milk, oil and honey together well. Add this mixture to the dry ingredients. Stir until just moistened. Fill greased or paper-lined muffin pans 2/3 full. Bake for 18 minutes, or until golden brown. Makes 10 muffins.

PARMESAN ALMOND MUFFINS

2 cups Quick Mix (see page 10)
1/2 cup grated Parmesan cheese
1/4 cup sugar
1 egg, well beaten
3/4 cup milk

ALMOND TOPPING:
2 tbs. butter **or** margarine
1 tsp. Worcestershire sauce
1/4 tsp. garlic salt
1/3 cup sliced almonds

Preheat oven to 400°F. Stir together Quick Mix, Parmesan cheese and sugar. Mix egg and milk together well. Add this mixture to dry ingredients. Stir until just moistened. Fill greased or paper-lined muffin pans 2/3 full. Prepare topping by melting butter in saucepan. Stir in remaining topping ingredients. Sprinkle topping over batter, pressing almonds into the batter slightly. Bake for 18 minutes, or until golden brown. Makes 12 muffins.

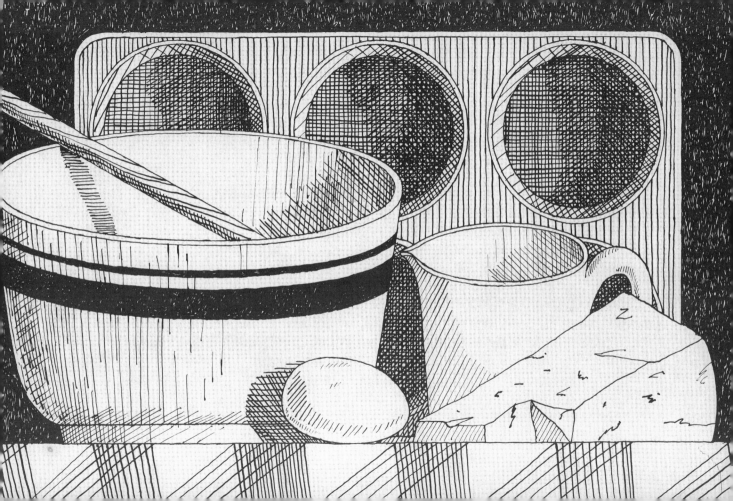

PEANUT BUTTER BACON MUFFINS

Kids don't have to wait until lunchtime to enjoy one of their favorite flavors! Bacon adds a nutritional bonus, and jelly added after baking will complete a tried and true duo.

1-1/2 cups all purpose flour
2-1/2 tsp. baking powder
1 cup whole wheat flakes, crushed
3 slices bacon, fried and crumbled
1/3 cup sugar

1 egg, well beaten
1 cup milk
2 tbs. oil
1/2 cup chunky peanut butter

Preheat oven to 400°F. Stir together flour, baking powder, whole wheat flakes, bacon and sugar. Mix egg, milk, oil and peanut butter together well. Add this mixture to dry ingredients. Stir until just moistened. Fill greased or paper-lined muffin pans 2/3 full. Bake for 18 minutes, or until golden brown. Makes 12 muffins.

RYE CARAWAY MUFFINS

Ham and cheese on a sliced rye caraway muffin is a "deli" delight!

1 cup whole wheat **or** all purpose flour
1 cup rye flour
2-1/2 tsp. baking powder
1/2 tsp. baking soda
1/2 tsp. salt
2 tbs. sugar
2 tsp. caraway seed
1 egg, well beaten
1 cup buttermilk
1/4 cup oil

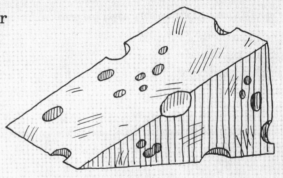

Preheat oven to 400°F. Stir together flour, rye flour, baking powder, baking soda, salt, sugar and caraway seeds. Mix egg, buttermilk and oil together well. Add mixture to the dry ingredients. Stir until just moistened. Fill greased or paper-lined muffin pans 2/3 full. Bake 18 minutes, or until done. Makes 12 muffins.

CHILI CORN MUFFINS

Don't wait for mañana to try these!

1/3 cup unbleached all purpose flour
1-1/3 cups yellow cornmeal
2 tsp. baking powder
1/2 tsp baking soda
1/2 tsp. salt
2 tbs. sugar
1/2 tsp. chili powder
3 tbs. green chilies, chopped

1 egg, well beaten
1/3 cup milk
2 tbs. oil
1 cup sour cream
12 thin slices Cheddar
or Monterey Jack cheese (optional)
1/4 cup poppy seeds (optional)

Preheat oven to 400°F. Stir together flour, cornmeal, baking powder, baking soda, salt, sugar, chili powder and chilies. Mix egg, milk, oil and sour cream together well. Add this mixture to dry ingredients. Stir until just moistened. Let batter rest for 5 minutes. Fill greased or paper-lined muffin pans 2/3 full. If desired, top each muffin with a thin slice of cheese and sprinkle with poppy seeds. Bake for 20 minutes, or until golden brown. Makes 16 muffins.

ZUCCHINI CHEESE MUFFINS

These flavorful muffins will enhance a soup, salad or hot dinner. We like to bake them in mini muffin pans and serve them as hors d'oeuvres, too!

2 cups all purpose flour
1 tbs. baking powder
1/2 tsp. salt
2 tbs. sugar
2 tbs. minced onion
3 slices of bacon, fried and crumbled

1/2 cup grated sharp Cheddar cheese
3/4 cup shredded zucchini
1 egg, well beaten
3/4 cup milk
1/4 cup oil

Preheat oven to 400°F. Stir together flour, baking powder, salt, sugar, onion, bacon, cheese and zucchini. Mix egg, milk and oil together well. Add this mixture to dry ingredients. Stir until just moistened. Fill greased or paper-lined muffin pans 2/3 full. Bake for 20 minutes, or until golden brown. Makes 12 muffins.

QUICK SWEET MUFFINS

This variation of our Quick Mix provides a basic sweet muffin. See page 35 for variations.

2 cups Quick Mix (see page 10)
1/2 cup sugar or honey
1/2 cup milk when using honey (2/3 cup milk when using sugar)
1 egg, well beaten

Preheat oven to 400°F. Mix sugar **or** honey, milk and egg together well. Add this mixture to Quick Mix. Stir until just moistened. Fill greased or paper lined muffin pans 2/3 full. Bake for 20 minutes, or until golden brown. Makes 10 muffins.

BASIC SWEET MUFFINS

This delicate muffin is ideal for many variations. Children love the surprise of jam baked inside (see page 35).

3/4 cup whole wheat flour
1 cup unbleached all purpose flour } **or** 1-3/4 cups all purpose flour
2-1/2 tsp. baking powder
1/2 tsp. salt
1/2 cup milk when using honey (3/4 cup milk when using sugar)
1 egg, well beaten
1/3 cup oil
1/2 cup honey **or** sugar

Preheat oven to 400°F. Stir together flour, baking powder and salt. Mix milk, egg, oil and honey **or** sugar together well. Add this mixture to dry ingredients. Stir until just moistened. Let sit for one minute. Fill greased or paper-lined muffin pans 2/3 full. Bake for 20 minutes, or until golden brown. Makes 12 muffins.

SWEET MUFFIN VARIATIONS

Add one of the following to the dry ingredients:

* 1/2 cup chopped walnuts
* 1/2 cup raisins
* 1/2 cup peeled and cored apple, grated
* 1 cup blueberries (rinsed well and patted dry, if they are canned or frozen)
* 1 tbs. grated orange **or** lemon peel
* Place one teaspoon of jam or marmalade on top of each muffin before baking. Or, fill muffin cups 1/2 full with batter and drop one teaspoon of jam or one slice of banana on each, then fill to 2/3 full with batter.
* Streusel Topping

  3 tbs. flour (whole wheat or all purpose)   1/4 tsp. nutmeg
  1/4 cup brown sugar, firmly packed   1/4 cup chopped pecans or walnuts
  1/2 tsp. cinnamon   2 tbs. butter **or** margarine

  Combine flour, brown sugar, cinnamon, nutmeg and chopped nuts. Cut butter into dry ingredients until mixture is crumbly. Sprinkle topping mixture on muffin batter before baking.

APPLE RAISIN MUFFINS

For all you apple lovers, this muffin has a tempting, spicy apple flavor.

2 cups Quick Mix (see page 10)
1/2 tsp. cinnamon
1/2 cup raisins
1/2 cup brown sugar, firmly packed
1/2 cup peeled and cored apple, grated
1 egg, well beaten
1/2 cup milk

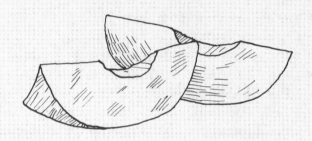

Preheat oven to 400°F. Combine Quick Mix, cinnamon, raisins, brown sugar and grated apple. Mix egg and milk together well. Add this mixture to dry ingredients. Stir until just moistened. Fill greased or paper-lined muffin pans 2/3 full. Bake for 20 minutes, or until golden brown. Makes 12 muffins.

BANANA OATMEAL MUFFINS

Wake up your family with the mouth-watering aroma of these breakfast muffins.

1-1/2 cups all purpose flour
1 cup quick-cooking oatmeal
2 tsp. baking powder
1 tsp. baking soda
1/2 tsp. salt
1 egg, well beaten

1/2 cup milk when using honey
  (3/4 cup milk when using sugar)
1/3 cup oil
1/2 cup honey **or** sugar
2/3 cup mashed banana

Preheat oven to 400°F. Stir together flour, oatmeal, baking powder, baking soda, and salt. Mix egg, milk, oil, honey **or** sugar and mashed banana together well. Add this mixture to dry ingredients. Stir until just moistened. Fill greased or paper-lined muffin pans 2/3 full. Bake for 20 minutes, or until golden brown. Makes about 16 muffins.

BLUEBERRY GINGER MUFFINS

Try this delicious and unusual combination.

2-1/2 cups all purpose flour
1 tbs. baking powder
1/2 tsp. baking soda
1/2 tsp. salt
1/3 cup sugar
1 tsp. cinnamon
1/2 tsp. ginger

1 egg, well beaten
1 cup buttermilk
1/4 cup oil
1/2 cup dark molasses
1 cup blueberries (rinsed well and patted dry,
   if they are canned or frozen)

Preheat oven to 400°F. Stir together flour, baking powder, baking soda, salt, sugar, cinnamon, and ginger. Mix egg, buttermilk, oil, and molasses together well. Add this mixture to dry ingredients. Stir until just moistened. Gently fold in blueberries. Fill greased or paper-lined muffin pans 2/3 full. Bake for 20 minutes, or until done. Makes 18 muffins.

CAROB COCONUT MUFFINS

1 cup whole wheat flour
3/4 cup unbleached all purpose flour } **or** 1-3/4 cup all purpose flour
1/4 cup carob **or** unsweetened cocoa powder
2-1/2 tsp. baking powder
1/2 tsp. salt
1/2 tsp. cinnamon
1/3 cup chopped pecans **or** walnuts
1/3 cup flaked coconut
1 egg, well beaten
3/4 cup milk
1/3 cup oil
1/2 cup honey

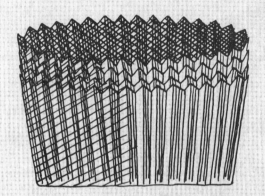

Preheat oven to 400ºF. Stir together flour, carob powder, baking powder, salt, cinnamon, nuts and coconut. Mix egg, milk, oil and honey together well. Add this mixture to dry ingredients. Stir until just moistened. Fill greased or paper-lined muffin pans 2/3 full. Bake for 20 minutes, or until done. Makes 12 muffins.

COCONUT PINEAPPLE MUFFINS

These muffins are as light as a tropical breeze.

2 cups all purpose flour
1 tbs. baking powder
1/2 tsp. salt
1/2 cup **each** sugar and
    flaked coconut
1 egg, well beaten

1/4 cup oil
1/3 cup milk
1 tsp. vanilla
1 can (8 oz.) of crushed pineapple, undrained
1 small package of sliced almonds (optional)

Preheat oven to 400°F. Stir together flour, baking powder, salt, sugar and coconut. Mix egg, oil, milk, vanilla and pineapple together well. Add this mixture to dry ingredients. Stir until just moistened. Fill greased or paper-lined muffin pans 2/3 full. If desired, sprinkle sliced almonds over batter and press them in lightly. Bake for 20 minutes, or until golden brown. Makes about 14 muffins.

CRANBERRY ORANGE MUFFINS

These muffins make a perfect accompaniment to a holiday dinner.

2 cups Quick Mix (see page 10)
1/2 cup sugar
1 tbs. grated orange rind
1/2 cup chopped pecans **or** walnuts
1 egg, well beaten
1/4 cup orange juice
1 can (8 oz.) whole cranberry sauce

Preheat oven to 400°F. Stir together Quick Mix, sugar, grated orange rind and chopped nuts. Mix egg, orange juice and cranberry sauce together well. Add this mixture to dry ingredients. Stir until just moistened. Fill greased or paper-lined muffin pans 2/3 full. Bake for 25 minutes, or until golden brown. Makes 12 muffins.

LEMON YOGURT MUFFINS

Lemon yogurt is our choice for this moist muffin. Be inventive and substitute your favorite yogurt flavor.

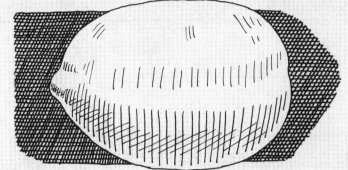

2 cups all purpose flour
2-1/2 tsp. baking powder
1/2 tsp. **each** baking soda and salt
1 tbs. grated lemon peel
1 egg, well beaten
1/4 cup oil
1/3 cup honey
1 carton (8 oz.) lemon yogurt

Preheat oven to 400°F. Stir together flour, baking powder, baking soda, salt and grated lemon peel. Mix egg, oil, honey and yogurt together well. Add this mixture to dry ingredients. Stir until just moistened. A few lumps from yogurt will remain. Fill greased or paper-lined muffin pans 2/3 full. Bake for 18 minutes, or until golden brown. Makes 12 muffins.

SANDWICH LOAVES, DINNER BREADS, AND SWEET LOAVES

Delight your family and friends with the moist, flavorful goodness of homemade quick breads by the loaf. If you like the idea of giving something homemade at Christmas time, what better gift than one of our sweet loaves (see pages 59 through 87). Wrap the bread in bright red or green cellophane and tie it with a bow.

These "helpful hints" should make baking quick breads by the loaf fun and easy for you.

• Like muffins, loaf batter should not be overmixed. When you combine liquid and dry ingredients, try to use as few strokes as possible.

• If the recipe calls for butter or margarine, allow it to soften at room temperature for a few hours before you use it. Then, beat it until it becomes creamy.

• If you always grease and flour your pans, loaves will turn out of them easily.

• Check your bread half-way through its baking time. If the top has become too brown, cover it with aluminum foil for the rest of baking time.

• The loaf is done if a toothpick inserted into the thickest part comes out clean.

• Cool the bread in its pan for about ten minutes. Then remove from pan and cool completely on a wire rack.

• Your bread will stay fresh longer if you wrap it securely in aluminum foil.

46

COTTAGE CHEESE LOAF

1-1/2 cups whole wheat flour
1-1/2 cups unbleached all purpose flour } **or** 3 cups all purpose flour
1 tbs. baking powder
1/2 tsp. **each** salt and dill
1/4 cup chopped green onion (optional)
1 tbs. sugar
1 cup milk
1 egg, well beaten
1/4 cup oil
1/2 cup cottage cheese

Preheat oven to 350°F. Stir together flour, baking powder, salt, dill, green onion and sugar. Mix milk, egg, oil and cottage cheese together well. Add this mixture to dry ingredients. Stir until just blended. Spread batter into a well-greased and floured loaf pan (9 x 5 x 3 inches). Bake for 1 hour and 10 minutes, or until done. Cool in pan for about 5 minutes, then turn out on a wire rack. Makes 1 loaf.

MEXICAN CORN BREAD

A perfect accompaniment to any South-of-the-Border meal. Try it with our chili on page 179.

1/2 cup whole wheat flour
1/2 cup unbleached all purpose flour } **or** 1 cup all purpose flour
3/4 cup yellow cornmeal
1 tbs. baking powder
1/2 tsp. salt
1 tsp. chili powder
2 tbs. minced onion
1/4 cup chopped green chilies (optional)
1 cup Mexican-style whole kernel corn, drained
1 cup shredded Cheddar cheese
1 cup milk
1 egg, well beaten
2 tbs. **each** oil and honey

Preheat oven to 400°F. Stir together flour, cornmeal, baking powder, salt, chili powder, onion, chilies, corn and cheese. Mix milk, egg, oil and honey together well. Add this mixture to dry ingredients. Stir until just blended. Let rest for 5 minutes. Pour batter into a greased (9 x 9 x 2 inch) baking pan. Bake for 25 minutes, or until golden brown. Makes 8 servings.

HEALTH BREAD

Bring them home for lunch with cream cheese and chopped olives between two slices of Health Bread.

3/4 cup soy flour
1 cup whole wheat flour
1 cup unbleached all purpose flour } **or** 2 cups all purpose flour
1/2 cup wheat germ
1/4 cup bran flakes
1/3 cup powdered milk
1 tbs. baking powder
1 tbs. baking soda
1/2 tsp. salt
1/2 cup **each** chopped dates **or** raisins, and chopped nuts (optional).
1 cup yogurt
1 egg, well beaten
1/4 cup **each** oil, molasses and honey
1/2 cup orange juice

50

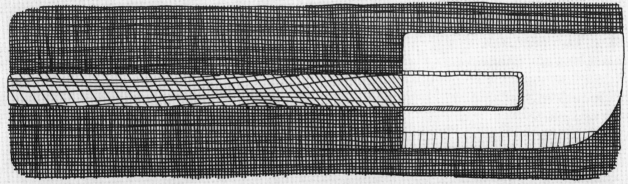

Preheat oven to 350°F. Stir together soy flour, wheat flour, wheat germ, bran, powdered milk, baking powder, baking soda, salt, dates and nuts. Mix yogurt, egg, oil, molasses, honey and orange juice together well. Add this mixture to dry ingredients. Stir until just blended. Spread batter into a greased and floured loaf pan (9 x 5 x 3 inches). Bake for one hour, or until done. Cover loosely with foil during the last 15 minutes of baking to prevent excess browning. Cool in pan for about 5 minutes, then turn out on a wire rack. Makes 1 loaf.

MOCK SOUR DOUGH BREAD

Great with dinner. Even better the next morning made into French Toast.

12 oz. can beer, flat
2 tbs. sugar **or** honey
3 cups unbleached all purpose flour
2 tsp. baking soda
1/2 tsp. salt
1 tbs. butter or margarine, melted

Preheat oven to 325°F. Combine beer and sugar in a large bowl. Mix in flour, baking soda and salt. Spread batter into a greased and floured loaf pan (9 x 5 x 3 inches). Bake for 50 minutes, or until done. Cool in pan for about 5 minutes, then turn out on a wire rack. Brush top of loaf with butter. Makes 1 loaf.

RAISIN OATMEAL BREAD

Tired of that same old boring bowl of oatmeal for breakfast? Try Raisin Oatmeal Bread instead.

2 cups all purpose flour
1 cup quick cooking oatmeal
1 tbs. baking powder
1/2 tsp. **each** baking soda and salt
1 cup raisins
1-1/4 cups buttermilk
1 egg, well beaten
1/4 cup **each** molasses and oil

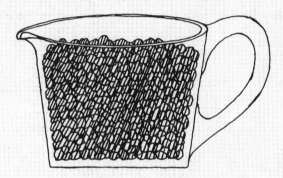

Preheat oven to 350ºF. Stir together flour, oatmeal, baking powder, baking soda, salt and raisins. Mix buttermilk, egg, molasses and oil together well. Add this mixture to dry ingredients. Stir until just blended. Pour batter into a greased and floured loaf pan (9 x 5 x 3 inches). Bake for 60 minutes, or until done. Cool in pan for about 5 minutes, then turn out on a wire rack. Makes 1 loaf.

RYE CHEESE BREAD

No need to go out to enjoy a "deli" sandwich. Mound thinly sliced ham or pastrami between two slices of this bread.

1 cup **each** rye flour and unbleached all purpose flour
1 tbs. baking powder
1/2 tsp. salt
1 tsp. dill
1 tbs. caraway seeds

1 cup **each** shredded
    Swiss cheese and milk
1 egg, well beaten
1/4 cup oil
2 tbs. honey

Preheat oven to 350°F. Stir together rye flour, all purpose flour, baking powder, salt, dill, caraway seeds and cheese. Mix milk, egg, oil and honey together well. Add this mixture to dry ingredients. Stir until just blended. Pour batter into a greased and floured loaf pan (9 x 5 x 3 inches). Bake for 55 minutes, or until done. Cool in pan for about 5 minutes, then turn out on a wire rack. Makes 1 loaf.

PIZZA BREAD

A meal in itself. Pizza bread can double for hor's d'oeuvres when cut into small squares.

1 cup whole wheat flour
1 cup unbleached all purpose flour } or 2 cups all purpose flour
1 tbs. baking powder
1/2 tsp. salt
1-1/2 tsp. oregano   **PIZZA SAUCE**
3/4 cup milk
1 egg, well beaten   1 can (6 oz.) tomato paste
1/4 cup oil   1/4 tsp. basil
1 tbs. honey   1/4 tsp. oregano
Topping (see next page) 1/4 tsp. garlic powder

Preheat oven to 400°F. Stir together flour, baking powder, salt and oregano. Mix milk, egg, oil and honey together well. Add this mixture to dry ingredients. Stir until just blended. Spread batter in a greased baking pan (9 x 9 x 2 inches).

Combine all ingredients for Pizza sauce. Spread on batter and cover with any combination of the topping ingredients. Bake for 30 minutes, or until done. Makes 4 servings.

TOPPING

1/2 cup sliced mushrooms
1/2 cup sliced green peppers
1/4 cup sliced black olives
5 diced anchovies
1/4 cup sliced onions

1/2 cup of any of the following:
  pepperoni, cooked Italian sausage,
  prosciutto, salami, **or** cooked ground beef
  (**or** 1/4 cup of any two).
1 cup shredded Mozarella cheese

Top pizza with mushrooms, green pepper, olives, anchovies and onions. Sprinkle meat on top of these ingredients. Top with Mozarella.

BANANA NUT BREAD

1/3 cup butter **or** margarine, softened
3/4 cup sugar
1 egg, well beaten
1 cup mashed banana
2 cups all purpose flour
2-1/2 tsp. baking powder

1/4 tsp. baking soda
1/2 tsp. salt
1 cup chopped pecans or walnuts
1/2 cup chocolate chips (optional)
1/2 cup buttermilk

Preheat oven to 350°F. Cream butter and sugar. Mix in egg and banana. Stir together flour, baking powder, baking soda, salt, nuts and chocolate chips. Add this mixture to the creamed mixture alternately with the buttermilk. Stir until just blended. Pour this mixture into a greased and floured loaf pan (9 x 5 x 3 inches). Bake for 65 minutes, or until done. Cool in pan for about 5 minutes, then turn out on a wire rack. Makes 1 loaf.

BASIC NUT BREAD

This classic nut bread lends itself to variations.

1 cup whole wheat flour
1 cup unbleached all purpose flour } **or** 2 cups all purpose flour
1 tbs. baking powder
1/2 tsp. salt
1 cup chopped pecans or walnuts
2/3 cup honey **or** 3/4 cup sugar
3/4 cup milk when using honey (1 cup milk when using sugar)
1 egg, well beaten
1/4 cup oil

Preheat oven to 350°F. Stir together flour, baking powder, salt and nuts. Mix honey, milk, egg and oil together well. Add this mixture to dry ingredients. Stir until just blended. Pour batter into a greased and floured loaf pan (9 x 5 x 3 inches). Bake for 50 minutes, or until done. Cool in pan for about 5 minutes, then turn out on a wire rack. Makes 1 loaf.

VARIATIONS FOR NUT BREAD

Use these variations to make all your holiday gift breads.

- **Date Nut Bread** Substitute 3/4 cup brown sugar for 3/4 cup sugar and add 1/2 cup chopped dates.

- **Orange Nut Bread** Substitute orange juice for milk and add 2 tablespoons grated orange peel.

- **Lemon Nut Bread** Add 1 tablespoon grated lemon peel.

- **Spice Nut Bread** Add 1/4 teaspoon cloves, plus 1/2 teaspoon **each** of cinnamon and nutmeg.

- **Pecan, Almond and Walnut Bread** Replace 1 cup chopped nuts with 1/3 cup **each** of chopped pecans, almonds and walnuts.

BOURBON BREAD

Serve this to your yuletide party guests.

2 cups unbleached all purpose flour
2-1/2 tsp. baking powder
1/2 tsp. baking soda
1/2 tsp. salt
1-1/2 tsp. mace or nutmeg
1 cup chopped pecans **or** walnuts

1 cup sugar
1 cup sour cream
1 egg, well beaten
1/4 cup oil
1/2 cup bourbon

Preheat oven to 350°F. Stir together flour, baking powder, baking soda, salt, mace, nuts and sugar. Mix sour cream, egg, oil and bourbon together well. Add this mixture to dry ingredients. Stir until just blended. Pour batter into a greased and floured loaf pan (9 x 5 x 3 inches), or into three greased and floured small loaf pans (6 x 3 x 2 inches). If desired, sprinkle batter with sugar before baking. Bake one standard loaf for 1 hour, or until done. Bake three small loaves for 45 minutes, or until done. Cool in pan for about 5 minutes, then turn out on a wire rack. Makes 1 large loaf, or three small loaves.

CHEDDAR BEER BREAD

Beer gives this bread a slightly sourdough flavor.

2-1/2 cups all purpose flour
1-1/2 tsp. baking soda
1/2 tsp. **each** salt and nutmeg
3/4 cup brown sugar, firmly packed
1 cup **each** raisins, shredded cheddar cheese and chopped pecans **or** walnuts
1-1/4 cup beer
1 egg, well beaten
1/4 cup oil

Preheat oven to 350°F. Stir together flour, baking soda, salt, nutmeg, brown sugar, raisins, cheese and nuts. Mix beer, egg and oil together well. Add this mixture to dry ingredients. Stir until just blended. Pour batter into a greased and floured loaf pan (9 x 5 x 3 inches). Bake for 60 minutes, or until done. Cool in pan for about 5 minutes, then turn out on a wire rack. Makes 1 loaf.

BRAN APPLESAUCE LOAF

If you need a mid-morning "pick me up," try a slice of this nutritious bread.

1/2 cup all bran cereal
1 cup applesauce
1/2 cup butter **or** margarine, softened
3/4 cup honey
1 egg, well beaten
2 cups all purpose flour

2 tsp. baking powder
1 tsp. baking soda
1/2 tsp. salt
1 tsp. cinnamon
1/4 tsp. cloves
1/2 cup raisins

Preheat oven to 350°F. Combine all bran cereal and applesauce. Set aside. Cream butter and honey. Add egg and mix well. Stir together flour, baking powder, baking soda, salt, cinnamon and cloves. Add dry mixture to creamed mixture alternately with applesauce and bran cereal. Mix until just blended. Stir in raisins. Pour batter into a greased and floured loaf pan (9 x 5 x 3 inches). Bake for 60 minutes, or until done. Cool in pan for about 5 minutes, then turn out on a wire rack. Makes 1 loaf.

HONEY BREAD

A moist bread spiced with cinnamon and ginger.

2 cups all purpose flour
1 tbs. baking powder
1/2 tsp. salt
1/2 tsp. cinnamon
1/4 tsp. ginger
1 egg, well beaten
3/4 cup milk
1/4 cup oil
1/2 cup honey

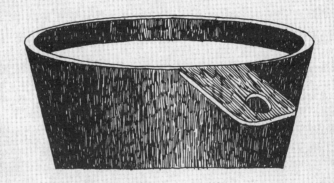

Preheat oven to 350°F. Stir together flour, baking powder, salt, cinnamon and ginger. Mix egg, milk, oil and honey together well. Add this mixture to the dry ingredients. Stir until just blended. Pour batter into a greased and floured loaf pan (9 x 5 x 3 inches). Bake for 50 minutes, or until done. Cool in pan about 5 minutes, then turn the loaf out on a wire rack. Makes 1 loaf.

BUTTERSCOTCH POPPY SEED LOAF

1/4 cup butter **or** margarine, softened
1 cup dark brown sugar, firmly packed
1 egg, well beaten
2 tsp. vanilla
2 cups all purpose flour
2 tsp. baking powder
1 tsp. baking soda
1/2 tsp. salt
3 tbs. poppy seeds
1 cup buttermilk

Preheat oven to 350°F. Cream butter and sugar. Stir in egg and vanilla. Combine flour, baking powder, baking soda, salt and poppy seeds. Add this mixture to creamed mixture alternately with the buttermilk. Stir until just blended. Pour batter into a greased and floured loaf pan (9 x 5 x 3 inches). Bake for 60 minutes, or until done. Cool in pan for about 5 minutes, then turn out on a wire rack. Makes 1 loaf.

CHRISTMAS FRUITCAKE

No need to spend hours in the kitchen baking your holiday fruitcake. This recipe is a snap to prepare. The longer you "mellow" your fruitcake, the better it tastes.

1-1/2 cups **each** whole almonds and walnut halves
1 lb. whole pitted dates
1 cup whole maraschino cherries, drained
1/2 cup candied orange peel
1/2 cup candied lemon peel
3/4 cup unbleached all purpose flour
3/4 cup sugar
1/2 tsp. baking powder
1/2 tsp. salt
3 eggs, well beaten
1 tsp. vanilla
1/4 cup brandy (more if desired)
wax paper, cheese cloth and aluminum foil

Preheat oven to 300°F. In a large bowl, combine almonds, walnuts, dates, cherries, orange peel and lemon peel. Stir together flour, sugar, baking powder and salt. Add dry mixture to the nut and fruit mixture. Beat eggs and vanilla together. Add them to nut, fruit and flour mixture. Mix thoroughly. Grease a 9 x 5 x 3 inch loaf pan. Line bottom and long sides with waxed paper; grease the paper. Pour batter into pan and press it into corners. Bake for two hours, or until done. Cool in pan for 10 minutes. Spoon 1/4 cup brandy over fruitcake. Remove from pan. Peel off waxed paper, and cool completely on wire rack. Wrap loosely in several layers of cheese cloth. Then, wrap tightly in aluminum foil. Refrigerate for at least 24 hours before slicing. You may mellow the fruitcake for up to 3 months before serving. If you do this, be sure to keep the fruitcake refrigerated at all times, and continue to spoon 1/4 cup of brandy over the cake every other week. In this way, it will remain moist. When serving, slice thinly. Makes 1 loaf.

MORAGA PEAR AND WALNUT BREAD

Living in the midst of pear and walnut orchards in Moraga, California, we were inspired to create this recipe.

1 cup whole wheat flour
1 cup unbleached all purpose flour } or 2 cups all purpose flour
1 tbs. baking powder
1/2 tsp. salt
1/2 tsp. cinnamon
1/4 tsp. nutmeg
1/4 tsp. cloves
1 cup canned pears, drained and chopped
1 cup coarsely chopped walnuts
1/2 cup milk
1 egg, well beaten
1/4 cup oil
3/4 cup honey

Preheat oven to 350ºF. Stir together flour, baking powder, salt, cinnamon, nutmeg, cloves, pears and walnuts. Mix milk, egg, oil and honey together well. Add this mixture to dry ingredients. Stir until just blended. Pour batter into a greased and floured loaf pan (9 x 5 x 3 inches). Bake for 65 minutes, or until done. Cool in pan for about 5 minutes, then turn out on a wire rack. Makes 1 loaf.

PEANUT BUTTER BANANA BREAD

Chopped peanuts add extra nutrition to this bread. A slice will boost your energy any time of day.

1/2 cup crunchy peanut butter
1/4 cup oil
1/2 cup honey
1 egg, well beaten
1 cup mashed banana
2 cups whole wheat flour

1 cup wheat germ
1 tbs. baking powder
1/2 tsp. salt
1/2 cup chopped peanuts (optional)
3/4 cup milk

Preheat oven to 350°F. Mix peanut butter, oil, honey, egg and mashed banana together well. Combine flour, wheat germ, baking powder, salt and peanuts. Add dry mixture to liquid ingredients alternately with the milk. Spread batter in a greased and floured loaf pan (9 x 5 x 3 inches). Bake for 1 hour, or until done. Cool in pan for about 5 minutes, then turn out on a wire rack. Makes 1 loaf.

PINEAPPLE COTTAGE CHEESE LOAF

This bread becomes dessert when served with Tropical Fruit Spread (see page 175).

1/2 cup butter **or** margarine, softened
3/4 cup honey
2 eggs, well beaten
2 cups all purpose flour
1 tbs. baking powder
1/2 tsp. salt
1 can (8 ozs.) drained crushed pineapple
1/2 cup cottage cheese

Preheat oven to 350°F. Cream butter and honey. Add eggs and mix thoroughly. Stir together flour, baking powder and salt. Add dry mixture to creamed mixture alternately with pineapple and cottage cheese. Pour batter into a greased and floured loaf pan (9 x 5 x 3 inches). Bake for 65 minutes, or until done. Cool in pan for about 5 minutes, then turn out on a wire rack. Makes 1 loaf.

SWEET POTATO BREAD

1 cup whole wheat flour
1 cup unbleached all purpose flour } **or** 2 cups all purpose flour
1 tbs. baking powder
1/2 tsp. salt
1 cup sugar
1/4 tsp. ginger
1/2 tsp. cinnamon
1/4 tsp. nutmeg
1/2 cup chopped pecans **or** walnuts
1/2 cup orange juice
1 egg, well beaten
1/3 cup oil
16 oz. can sweet potatoes **or** yams, drained and mashed (1-1/3 cups)

Preheat oven to 350°F. Combine flour, baking powder, salt, sugar, ginger, cinnamon, nutmeg and nuts. Mix orange juice, egg, oil and sweet potatoes together well. Add this mixture to dry ingredients. Stir until just blended. Pour batter into a greased and floured loaf pan (9 x 5 x 3 inches). Bake for 1 hour and 15 minutes, or until done. Cool in pan for about 5 minutes, then turn out on a wire rack. Makes 1 loaf.

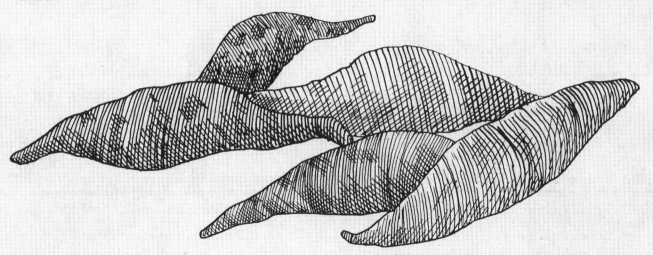

TOASTED COCONUT BREAD

Toasting the coconut enchances this bread's nut-like flavor.

1 cup shredded coconut
2 cups unbleached all purpose flour
1 tbs. baking powder
1/2 tsp. salt
1 cup milk

1 egg, well beaten
1/4 cup oil
3/4 cup sugar
1 tsp. vanilla

Preheat oven to 350°F. Place coconut in a large, shallow baking pan in preheated oven. Stir occasionally, until it is golden brown (about 5 minutes). Stir together flour, baking powder and salt. Mix milk, egg, oil and vanilla together well. Add to the dry ingredients. Stir until just blended. Pour batter into a greased and floured loaf pan (9 x 5 x 3 inches). Bake for 1 hour, or until done. Cool in pan for about 5 minutes, then turn out on wire rack. Makes 1 loaf.

ZUCCHINI CARROT BREAD

Flecks of green and orange give this bread its lively appearance.

2 cups all purpose flour
1/2 cup **each** white sugar and brown sugar, firmly packed
1 tbs. baking powder
1/2 tsp. salt
1 tsp. cinnamon
1 cup **each** chopped pecans **or** walnuts, grated zucchini and grated carrots
1 egg, well beaten
1/3 cup oil
1/2 cup milk

Preheat oven to 350°F. Stir together flour, sugars, baking powder, salt, cinnamon, nuts, zucchini and carrots. Mix egg, oil and milk together well. Stir until just blended. Pour into a greased and floured loaf pan (9 x 5 x 3 inches). Bake for 70 minutes, or until done. Cool in pan for 5 minutes, then turn out on wire rack. Makes 1 loaf.

28 FAVORITE SWEET QUICK MIX LOAVES

Find your favorite flavor on our chart and bake a delicious Quick Mix loaf. With Quick Mix on hand (see page 10), you can prepare one or more loaves in no time, by simply following our basic directions.

Combine the dry ingredients. Mix the liquid ingredients together well. Add them to the dry ingredients. Stir until just blended. Pour the batter into a greased and floured loaf pan (9 x 5 x 3 inches). Bake in a preheated 350°F. oven, for 55 to 65 minutes, or until done. Or, bake in three small loaf pans (6 x 3 x 2 inches), for 45 to 50 minutes. Cool in the pan for about 5 minutes, then turn out on a wire rack.

Put on your thinking cap and be creative with our basic loaves. Add an unusual spice, like cardamon, ginger or anise. Mix and match different nuts, fruits and vegetables. Use either honey or sugar. We have included proportions for both. Take an old family favorite and improvise or create a new one!

	ALMOND	APPLE	APRICOT	BANANA
Quick Mix	3-1/2 cups	3-1/2 cups	3-1/2 cups	3-1/2 cups
Spices and Flavorings	1 tsp. almond extract	1 tsp. cinnamon		
Nuts	1 cup sliced almonds	1 cup chopped nuts	1 cup chopped nuts	1 cup chopped nuts
Variation		1 cup apple, shredded	1 cup diced, dried apricots	1 cup mashed banana
Egg	1	1	1	1
Honey and Liquid	2/3 cup honey and 1 cup milk	2/3 cup honey and 2/3 cup milk or apple juice	3/4 cup honey and 3/4 cup apricot nectar	2/3 cup honey 1/3 cup milk
OR				
Sugar and Liquid	3/4 cup sugar and 1-1/4 cup milk	3/4 cup brown sugar, firmly packed, and 1 cup milk or apple juice	1 cup sugar and 1 cup apricot nectar	3/4 cup sugar and 1/2 cup milk

	BLUEBERRY	BUTTER-SCOTCH CHIP	CARROT	CHOCOLATE OR CAROB CHIP
Quick Mix	3-1/2 cups	3-1/2 cups	3-1/2 cups	3-1/2 cups
Spices and Flavoring	1 tsp. grated orange peel	1 tsp. vanilla	1 tsp. cinnamon	
Nuts	1 cup chopped nuts	1 cup chopped nuts	1 cup chopped nuts	1 cup chopped nuts
Variation	1 cup blueberries	1 butter-scotch chips	1 cup grated carrot	1 cup chocolate or carob chips
Egg	1	1	1	1
Honey and Liquid	2/3 cup honey and 1 cup orange juice	2/3 cup honey and 1 cup milk	2/3 cup honey and 2/3 cup milk	2/3 cup honey and 1 cup milk
OR **Sugar and Liquid**	3/4 cup sugar and 1 cup orange juice	3/4 cup brown sugar, firmly packed, and 1-1/4 cups milk	3/4 cup brown sugar, firmly packed, and 1 cup milk	3/4 cup sugar and 1-1/4 cups milk

81

	COCONUT	CRANBERRY	DATE	FIG
Quick Mix	3-1/2 cups	3-1/2 cups	3-1/2 cups	3-1/2 cups
Spices and Flavorings		1 tbs. grated orange peel	1 tbs. grated orange peel	1/2 tsp. cinnamon and 1/2 tsp. all spice
Nuts	1 cup chopped nuts	1 cup chopped nuts	1 cup chopped nuts	1 cup chopped nuts
Variation	3/4 cup coconut	3/4 cup cranberries, chopped	1 cup dates, chopped	1 cup chopped, dried figs
Egg	1	1	1	1
Honey and Liquid	2/3 cup honey and 1 cup milk	2/3 cup honey and 3/4 cup orange juice	2/3 cup honey and 3/4 cup orange juice	2/3 cup honey and 3/4 cup orange juice
OR				
Sugar and Liquid	3/4 cup brown sugar, firmly packed, and 1-1/4 cups milk	3/4 cup brown sugar, firmly packed, and 1 cup orange juice	3/4 cup sugar and 1 cup orange juice	3/4 cup sugar and 1 cup orange juice

82

	GRANOLA	LEMON	ORANGE	PEACH
Quick Mix	3-1/2 cups	3-1/2 cups	3-1/2 cups	3-1/2 cups
Spices and Flavorings		2 tbs. grated lemon peel	2 tbs. grated orange peel	1 tsp. cinnamon
Nuts		1 cup chopped nuts	1 cup chopped nuts	1 cup chopped nuts
Variation	1 cup granola			1 cup diced, dried peaches
Egg	1	1	1	1
Honey and Liquid	2/3 cup honey and 1 cup milk, apple or orange juice	2/3 cup honey and 1 cup milk	2/3 cup honey and 1 cup orange juice	2/3 cup honey and 3/4 cup orange juice
OR **Sugar and Liquid**	3/4 cup sugar and 1-1/4 cups milk, apple or orange juice	3/4 cup sugar and 1-1/4 cups milk	3/4 cup sugar and 1-1/4 cups orange juice	3/4 cup sugar and 1 cup orange juice

83

	PEANUT	PEAR	PECAN	PINEAPPLE
Quick Mix	3-1/2 cups	3-1/2 cups	3-1/2 cups	3-1/2 cups
Spices and Flavorings		1 tsp. cinnamon		1 tbs. grated orange peel
Nuts	1 cup chopped peanuts	1 cup chopped nuts	1 cup chopped pecans	1 cup chopped nuts
Variation		1 cup diced, dried pears		2/3 cup drained crushed pineapple
Egg	1	1	1	1
Honey and Liquid	2/3 cup honey and 1 cup milk	2/3 cup honey and 3/4 cup orange juice	2/3 cup honey and 1 cup milk	2/3 cup honey and 2/3 cup orange juice
OR **Sugar and Liquid**	3/4 cup brown sugar, firmly packed, and 1-1/4 cups milk	3/4 cup sugar and 1 cup orange juice	3/4 cup brown sugar, firmly packed, and 1-1/4 cups milk	3/4 cup brown sugar, firmly packed, and 3/4 cup orange juice

	PRUNE	**PUMPKIN**	**RAISIN**	**SPICE**
Quick Mix	3-1/2 cups	3-1/2 cups	3-1/2 cups	3-1/2 cups
Spices and Flavorings	1 tbs. grated orange peel	1 tsp. cinnamon 1/2 tsp. allspice		1/2 tsp. cinnamon 1/2 tsp. nutmeg 1/4 tsp. cloves
Nuts	1 cup chopped nuts	1 cup chopped nuts	1 cup chopped nuts	1 cup chopped nuts
Variation	1 cup chopped, dried prunes	1 cup canned pumpkin	1 cup raisins	
Egg	1	1	1	1
Honey and Liquid **OR**	2/3 cup honey and 3/4 cup prune juice	2/3 cup honey and 1/3 cup milk	2/3 cup honey and 3/4 cup milk or orange juice	2/3 cup honey and 1 cup milk
Sugar and Liquid	3/4 cup sugar and 1 cup prune juice	3/4 cup sugar and 1/2 cup milk	3/4 cup sugar and 1 cup milk or orange juice	3/4 cup sugar and 1-1/4 cups milk

	SWEET POTATO OR YAM	WALNUT	YOGURT	ZUCCHINI
Quick Mix	3-1/2 cups	3-1/2 cups	3-1/2 cups	3-1/2 cups
Spices and Flavorings	1 tsp. cinnamon 1/2 tsp. allspice		1/2 tsp. baking soda	1 tsp. cinnamon
Nuts	1 cup chopped nuts	1 cup chopped walnuts	1 cup chopped nuts	1 cup chopped nuts
Variation	1 cup mashed, cooked sweet potato		1 cup yogurt, any flavor	1 cup shredded zucchini
Egg	1	1	1	1
Honey and Liquid	2/3 cup honey and 1/3 cup milk	2/3 cup honey and 1 cup milk	2/3 cup honey and 1/2 cup milk	2/3 cup honey and 2/3 cup milk
OR **Sugar and Liquid**	3/4 cup sugar and 1/2 cup milk	3/4 cup sugar and 1-1/4 cups milk	3/4 cup sugar and 2/3 cup milk	3/4 cup brown sugar, firmly packed, and 1 cup milk

BISCUITS

No pre-packaged baking mix can rival the flavor of homemade, fresh-baked biscuits. Spread with creamy butter and drizzled with honey, they are perfect with fried chicken or ham.

Here are a few suggestions that will help you produce delicious biscuits:

• The butter or margarine you use in your biscuits should be chilled, unlike the butter or margarine used in some loaf breads.

• Cut the butter or margarine into the dry ingredients using a pastry blender or two knives. Continue "cutting" until the mixture resembles coarse cornmeal.

• When you add the liquid to the dry ingredients, stir with a fork only until the mixture is moistened.

• To knead the dough, turn the mixture onto a floured surface and grasp the dough with both hands and gently push it away from you with the heals of your hands. Repeat this procedure ten to twelve times.

• Roll or pat the dough 1/2-inch thick. We like to roll our biscuits 1/4-inch thick and fold them over once before baking them. When they are done, they are much easier to split.

• For biscuits with soft sides, place them close together on a baking sheet. If

89

you prefer crisp biscuits, place them two inches apart on a baking sheet.
 • For a brown crust, brush tops of biscuits with milk before baking.

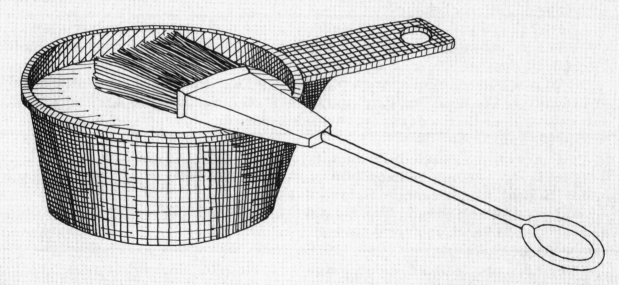

QUICK BISCUITS

The quickest of the quick. Just mix, bake and serve. Since these are so easy to put together, why not take a few minutes and add any of the variations on page 93.

2-1/2 cups Quick Mix (see page 10)
1/2 cup milk

Preheat oven to 450°F. Combine Quick Mix and milk. Knead gently twelve times. Roll or pat dough 1/2-inch thick, or 1/4-inch thick and fold over. Cut into squares, or 2-1/2 inch rounds. Bake on an ungreased baking sheet for 12 minutes, or until golden brown. Makes 10 biscuits.

For Drop Biscuits, decrease Quick Mix to 2 cups and combine with milk. Drop by tablespoonfuls onto a greased baking sheet. Bake for 10 to 12 minutes, or until golden brown. Makes 10 biscuits.

BASIC BAKING POWDER BISCUITS

These are the biscuits Grandma used to make.

1 cup whole wheat flour
1 cup unbleached all purpose flour $\Big\}$ **or** 2 cups all purpose flour
1 tbs. baking powder
1/2 tsp. salt
1/3 cup butter **or** margarine
3/4 cup milk

Preheat oven to 450°F. Stir together flour, baking powder and salt. Cut butter into dry ingredients until the mixture resembles coarse cornmeal. Add milk and stir slightly. Knead gently twelve times. Roll or pat dough 1/2-inch thick or roll 1/4-inch thick and fold over. Cut into squares, 2-1/2-inch rounds, or other interesting shapes with cookie cutters. Bake on an ungreased baking sheet for 12 minutes, or until golden brown. Makes 10 biscuits.

BASIC BISCUIT VARIATIONS

Create a different biscuit by adding one of the following to the dry ingredients:

- 3 tbs. crumbled bacon
- 1/4 cup snipped parsley
- 1/4 cup grated carrot
- 1/4 tsp. thyme, basil **or** marjoram
- 2 tsp. poppy, sesame **or** caraway seeds
- 3 tbs. grated onion
- 1/2 cup grated cheese
- 1/2 cup chopped nuts
- 1/2 cup chopped dates **or** raisins
- **Beverly's Buns**—Dip a sugar cube in orange juice and press into the center of each biscuit.
- **Drop Biscuits**—Increase the milk to 1 cup. Drop the batter by tablespoonfuls onto a greased baking sheet. Add any one of the above variations to the dry ingredients.

- **Filled Biscuits**—Roll the dough 1/4-inch thick. Spread any of the above variations or 1/4 teaspoon of jam on half of the dough; fold the other half over. Cut in squares or triangles.
- **Buttermilk Biscuits**—Replace the milk with buttermilk and add 1/2 teaspoon of baking soda.
- **Sour Cream Biscuits**—Substitute 1 cup of sour cream for the milk and add 1/2 teasspoon of baking soda.
- **Pinwheel Biscuits**—Roll the dough 1/4-inch thick, into a 10 x 16-inch rectangle. Brush with about 1/3 cup of melted butter or margarine and spread with any of the following variations below. Roll as for jelly roll (starting at the long end). Cut in 1-inch slices and bake. Makes 16 biscuits.

Variations:

1 cup grated cheese and 1/4 cup sliced ripe olives or sliced green onions

1/2 cup sugar and 1 tsp. cinnamon, combined

1/2 cup brown sugar, firmly packed, and 1/2 cup chopped pecans **or** walnuts

1/2 cup jam or marmalade

1/2 cup sugar, 1 tbs. grated orange peel and 1/3 cup currants

HERB CHEESE DROP BISCUITS

For a light meal, split these biscuits and top with our Ratatouille (page 177).

2 cups Quick Mix (see page 10)
1/4 tsp. dill
1/4 tsp. oregano
3/4 cup grated cheddar cheese
3/4 cup milk

Preheat oven to 450°F. Stir together Quick Mix, dill, oregano and cheese. Add milk and stir until moistened. Divide into 6 large drop biscuits. Bake on a greased baking sheet for 15 minutes, or until golden brown. Makes 6 large or 12 regular drop biscuits.

HEALTH DROP BISCUITS

Serve these nutritious little nuggets instead of cookies.

1 cup all purpose flour
1/2 cup soy flour
1/3 cup wheat germ
2 tbs. bran flakes
1/3 cup powdered milk
1 tbs. baking powder
1/2 tsp. baking soda
1/4 tsp. salt
1/3 cup butter **or** margarine
1/4 cup chopped dates **or** raisins (optional)
1/4 cup chopped nuts **or** sunflower seeds (optional)
1/2 cup plain yogurt
2 tbs. **each** molasses and honey
1/4 cup orange juice

Preheat oven to 400ºF. Stir together flour, soy flour, wheat germ, bran, powdered milk, baking powder, baking soda and salt. Cut butter into dry ingredients until the mixture resembles coarse cornmeal. If desired, add the chopped dates and nuts. Mix yogurt, molasses, honey and orange juice together well. Add this mixture to dry ingredients. Stir slightly until moistened. Drop by tablespoonfuls onto a greased baking sheet. Bake for 10 minutes, or until golden brown. Makes 16 drop biscuits.

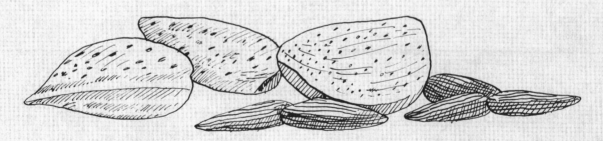

SWEET POTATO BISCUITS

3/4 cup whole wheat flour
3/4 cup unbleached all purpose flour } **or** 1-1/2 cups all purpose flour
2-1/2 tsp. baking powder
1/2 tsp. salt
1 tbs. brown sugar, firmly packed
1/3 cup butter **or** margarine
1/4 cup milk
1/2 cup cooked **or** canned sweet potato, mashed
1 tsp. cinnamon (optional)

Preheat oven to 425°F. Stir together flour, baking powder, salt and brown sugar. Cut butter into dry ingredients until the mixture resembles coarse cornmeal. Stir in milk and sweet potato. Knead gently twelve times. Roll or pat dough 1/2-inch thick, or 1/4-inch thick and fold over. Cut into 2-1/2-inch rounds. If desired, sprinkle with cinnamon. Bake on an ungreased baking sheet for 10 to 12 minutes, or until done. Makes about 10 biscuits.

RYE BISCUITS

When you go on your next picnic, use these biscuits instead of "regular" bread for mini sandwiches

1 cup **each** all purpose flour and rye flour
1 tbs. baking powder
1/2 tsp. **each** baking soda and salt
1 tbs. caraway seeds
1/3 cup butter **or** margarine
3/4 cup buttermilk

Preheat oven to 425°F. Stir together flours, baking powder, baking soda, salt and caraway seeds. Cut butter into dry ingredients until the mixture resembles coarse cornmeal. Add buttermilk and stir slightly. Knead dough gently twelve times. Roll or pat dough 1/2-inch thick, or 1/4-inch thick and fold over. Cut into squares, or 2-1/2-inch rounds. Bake on an ungreased baking sheet for 12 minutes, or until done. Makes 10 biscuits.

CORNMEAL BISCUITS

3/4 cup whole wheat flour
3/4 cup unbleached all purpose flour } **or** 1-1/2 cups all purpose flour
1/2 cup yellow cornmeal
2 tsp. baking powder
1/2 tsp. baking soda
1/2 tsp. salt
1/3 cup butter **or** margarine
1 cup sour cream
1 tbs. honey

Preheat oven to 450°F. Stir together the flour, cornmeal, baking powder, baking soda and salt. Cut butter into the mixture until it resembles coarse cornmeal. Add sour cream and honey. Stir slightly. Knead twelve times. Roll or pat dough 1/2-inch thick, or 1/4-inch thick and fold over. Cut into 2-1/2-inch rounds. If desired, sprinkle with paprika. Bake on an ungreased baking sheet for 10 minutes, or until golden brown. Makes 10 biscuits.

BREAD STICKS

A welcome addition to soups, salads or Italian dinners.

2 cups all purpose flour
1 tbs. baking powder
1/2 tsp. salt
1/4 cup butter **or** margarine

2 eggs, well beaten
1/3 cup milk
1/4 cup melted butter **or** margarine
2 tbs. sesame seeds (optional)

Preheat oven to 450°F. Stir together flour, baking powder and salt. Cut unmelted butter into dry ingredients until the mixture resembles coarse cornmeal. Mix together eggs and milk. Stir them into the dry mixture until moistened. Roll or pat the dough 1/2-inch thick in the shape of a rectangle of about 8 x 6-inches. Cut into sticks, 4 inches long and 1/2 inch wide. Roll gently to round the sides. Sprinkle with flour if the dough is too sticky to handle easily. Brush a cookie sheet with 1 tablespoon of the melted butter. Place bread sticks on the sheet and brush with remaining melted butter. If desired, sprinkle with sesame seeds. Bake for 12 minutes, or until golden brown. Makes 24 bread sticks.

CHEESE CORN STICKS

Instead of corn on the cob, serve Cheese Corn Sticks with your next barbecue.

1 cup all purpose flour
3/4 cup yellow cornmeal
1 tbs. baking powder
1/2 tsp. **each** baking soda and salt
1/2 cup shredded Cheddar **or** Monterey Jack cheese
1/4 cup honey **or** sugar
1 cup sour cream
1 egg, well beaten
2 tbs. oil

Preheat oven to 425°F. Stir together flour, cornmeal, baking powder, baking soda, salt and cheese. Mix honey, sour cream, egg and oil together well. Add this mixture to dry ingredients. Stir until just blended. Let batter rest for 5 minutes. Fill each greased section of the corn stick pan 2/3 full. Bake for 12 to 15 minutes, or until golden brown. Makes 18 corn sticks.

HANNAH'S RIESKA BREAD

Serve this traditional flat Finnish bread hot from the oven with butter.

1-1/2 cups unbleached all purpose flour
3/4 cup barley flour
1-1/2 tsp. baking powder
1/2 tsp. **each** baking soda and salt
2 tbs. sugar
1/4 cup butter **or** margarine
1 cup buttermilk

Preheat oven to 425°F. Stir together all purpose flour, barley flour, baking powder, baking soda, salt and sugar. Cut butter into dry ingredients until mixture resembles coarse cornmeal. Stir in buttermilk until a soft dough is formed. Roll or pat dough on a greased cookie sheet to make a 10-inch circle. Bake for 20 minutes, or until golden brown. Cut with a serrated knife. Makes 1 round loaf.

IRISH OATMEAL SODA BREAD

1-1/2 cups all purpose flour
1/2 cup quick cooking oatmeal
2-1/2 tsp. baking powder
1/2 tsp. baking soda
1/2 tsp. salt

2 tsp. caraway seeds
1 tbs. sugar
1/3 cup butter **or** margarine
1/2 cup currants **or** raisins
3/4 cup buttermilk

Preheat oven to 375°F. Stir together flour, oatmeal, baking powder, baking soda, salt, caraway seeds and sugar. Cut butter into dry ingredients until the mixture resembles coarse cornmeal. Stir in currants. Add buttermilk and stir until blended. Knead gently twelve times. Shape dough into a 7-inch wide circle on an ungreased baking sheet. Cut large "X" 1/4-inch deep across the top of entire dough. Bake for 30 minutes, or until golden brown. Cut in wedges to serve. Makes 1 loaf.

SWEET BISCUITS

2 cups all purpose flour
1 tbs. baking powder
1/2 tsp. salt
1/2 cup butter **or** margarine
3/4 cup cream
1 tbs. honey
1/4 cup milk
2 tbs. sugar

    Preheat oven to 450°F. Stir together flour, baking powder and salt. Cut the butter into the dry ingredients until the mixture resembles coarse cornmeal. Add cream and honey. Stir until blended. Knead gently twelve times. Roll or pat dough 1/2-inch thick, or 1/4-inch thick and fold over. Cut into 2-1/2-inch rounds. Brush with milk and sprinkle with sugar. Bake on an ungreased baking sheet for 12 minutes, or until golden brown. Makes 10 biscuits.

APPLE STRUDEL

An easy version of a classic dessert!

2 cups all purpose flour
1 tbs. baking powder
1/2 tsp. salt
1/3 cup butter **or** margarine
2/3 cup milk
2 tbs. melted butter **or** margarine
Filling (see page 109)
Glaze (see page 109)

Preheat oven to 400°F. Stir together flour, baking powder and salt. Cut butter into dry ingredients until the mixture resembles coarse cornmeal. Add milk and stir until blended. Knead gently twelve times. Roll dough to a 1/4-inch thick rectangle of about 10 x 6 inches. Brush with melted butter. Spread filling over dough. Roll as for jelly roll (starting at long end). Seal ends. Place on ungreased baking sheet in the shape of a crescent. Bake for 30 minutes, or until golden brown. Cool slightly, for about 5 minutes. Spread with glaze. Makes sixteen 1-inch slices.

FILLING

2 cups peeled, seeded, green cooking apples, thinly sliced
1/2 cup sugar
1 tsp. cinnamon

Mix all ingredients together well.

GLAZE

1/2 cup powdered sugar   1/4 tsp. vanilla
1 tbs. milk   1/2 cup chopped pecans **or** walnuts

Combine powdered sugar, milk and vanilla. Spread over Strudel. Sprinkle with nuts.

RAISIN NUT PINWHEELS

Our children love these for breakfast. They are so much better than the refrigerated variety of breakfast rolls.

2 cups Quick Mix (see page 10)
1/4 tsp. baking soda
1/2 cup raisins
1/2 cup sour cream
1/4 cup milk
1/4 cup melted butter

FILLING

1/4 cup brown sugar, firmly packed
2 tbs. wheat germ
1/4 cup chopped pecans **or** walnuts
1/2 tsp. cinnamon

Preheat oven to 450°F. Stir together Quick Mix, baking soda and raisins. Mix together sour cream and milk. Stir them into dry ingredients. Knead gently twelve times. Roll dough to a 1/4-inch thick rectangle of about 10 x 12 inches. Brush with melted butter. Combine filling ingredients. Sprinkle filling over dough. Roll as for jelly roll (starting at long end). Seal ends. Cut into 1-inch slices. Place cut side down on ungreased baking sheet. Bake for 12 minutes, or until golden brown. Makes 12 pinwheels.

SESAME SEED DROP BISCUITS

A blend of natural ingredients creates a wholesome biscuit.

1-1/2 cups whole wheat flour
1/2 cup wheat germ
1 tbs. baking powder
1/2 tsp. baking soda
1/2 tsp. salt
1/3 cup butter **or** margarine

1 egg, well beaten
1 cup buttermilk
1 tbs. honey **or** sugar
1/4 cup melted butter **or** margarine
1/2 cup sesame seeds

Preheat the oven to 400°F. Mix the flour, wheat germ, baking powder, baking soda and salt together. Cut in the butter until the mixture resembles coarse corn-meal. Combine the egg, buttermilk and honey. Stir this mixture into the dry ingredients. Drop by tablespoonfuls onto a greased baking sheet. Brush with melted butter, sprinkle with sesame seeds and bake 12 to 15 minutes. Makes 20 biscuits.

QUICK HOT CROSS BUNS

My family often requests them for a special birthday breakfast. These buns are traditionally served with Easter Brunch.

2 cups Quick Mix (see page 10)
1/4 cup currants **or** raisins
1/4 cup mixed candied fruit
1 tsp. cinnamon
1 tsp. instant coffee powder
1/4 cup sugar
1/2 cup milk
1 egg yolk
1 tbs. water
Frosting (see next page)

Preheat oven to 450°F. Stir together Quick Mix, currants, candied fruit, cinnamon, coffee powder and sugar. Add milk and stir to form a soft dough. Knead on a floured surface 25 times. Shape into 8 balls and place close together in a greased and floured 8-inch round baking pan. Combine egg yolk and water. Brush over tops of the buns. Bake for 15 minutes, or until golden brown. Cool and decorate with frosting.

FROSTING

1/3 cup powdered sugar
1 tsp. milk

Combine the ingredients. Decorate each bun with an "X." Makes 8 buns.

GRANOLA SCONES

1 cup whole wheat flour   } **or** 2 cups all purpose flour
1 cup unbleached all purpose flour
1 tbs. baking powder
1/2 tsp. salt
1/4 cup butter **or** margarine
1 cup granola
1/3 cup milk
2 eggs
2 tbs. honey **or** sugar

    Preheat oven to 400ºF. Stir together the flour, baking powder and salt. Cut butter into mixture until it resembles coarse cornmeal. Stir in granola. Combine milk, eggs and honey. Stir into dry ingredients until moistened. Knead fifteen times on a floured surface. Divide the dough in half and form two balls. Roll or pat each one 1/2-inch thick, forming 2 six-inch circles. Cut each circle into 6 wedges. Bake on an ungreased baking sheet for 15 minutes, or until golden brown. Makes 12 scones.

BASIC SCONES

Scones are a British invention which can be cut into a variety of shapes such as squares, diamonds, hearts or triangles. Serve hot from the oven with butter and jam, and to be completely authentic, tea.

1 cup whole wheat flour

1 cup unbleached all purpose flour } **or** 2 cups all purpose flour

1 tbs. baking powder

1/2 tsp. salt

6 tbs. butter **or** margarine

1/2 cup milk

1 egg, well beaten

2 tbs. honey **or** sugar

Preheat oven to 425°F. Mix together flour, baking powder and salt. Cut butter into dry ingredients until the mixture resembles coarse cornmeal. Combine milk, egg and honey. Stir them into dry ingredients until moistened. Knead fifteen times on a floured surface. Divide dough in half and form into two balls. Roll or pat each one 1/2-inch thick, forming 2 six-inch circles. Cut each circle into 6 wedges. Or, you may wish to pat the dough 1/2-inch thick and cut into squares, triangles or diamonds. Bake on an ungreased baking sheet for 12 minutes, or until golden brown.

For variety add 1/2 cup currants, raisins or chopped nuts to the dry ingredients. You may use buttermilk in place of milk and add 1/2 teaspoon of baking soda.

Grandpa Jack rolls his scones 1/4-inch thick, folds the dough over once, and cuts it into triangles. He brushes the top of the scones with egg white, then sprinkles them with sugar before baking.

BASIC SHORTCAKE

There is hardly any better base for fresh fruit than shortcake. Top with any fresh fruit in season and add a dollop of whipped cream for good measure.

1 cup whole wheat flour
1 cup unbleached all purpose flour } **or** 2 cups all purpose flour
1 tbs. baking powder
1/2 tsp. salt
1/2 cup butter **or** margarine
2/3 cup light cream
1 egg, well beaten
2 tbs. honey **or** sugar
1 tbs. sugar

Preheat oven to 450°F. Mix flour, baking powder and salt together. Cut butter into dry ingredients until the mixture resembles coarse cornmeal. Stir cream, egg and honey together well. Add them to the dry mixture. Stir until moistened. Pat dough into a greased and floured 8 x 8 x 2-inch square pan or a 8 x 1-1/2-inch round pan and sprinkle with sugar. Bake for 15 minutes, or until golden brown. Serve warm, split and filled with fruit and whipped cream.

For individual shortcakes prepare basic shortcake dough. Knead dough gently on a floured surface, then pat or roll 1/2-inch thick. Cut eight shortcakes with a 2-1/2-inch round cutter and sprinkle with sugar. Bake 8 to 10 minutes on an ungreased baking sheet. Serve as above.

COFFEE CAKES

Wake up your "sleepy heads" with an Apple Graham Coffee Cake. If there are any leftovers, serve squares of it with vanilla ice cream for dessert. If you have big plans for Sunday, but still would like to enjoy brunch, why not whip up a batch of Quick Mix coffee cake? There are ten toppings to choose from.

Here are a few hints to make your coffee cakes just a little bit more special:

• If the recipe calls for butter or margarine, allow it to soften at room temperature for a few hours before using it. Then, beat it until it becomes creamy.

• When adding the dry ingredients to the butter or margarine alternately with the liquid ingredients, be sure not to overmix.

• The coffee cake is done when a toothpick inserted into the middle comes out clean. It will also start to pull away from the sides of the pan.

QUICK COFFEE CAKE

For those hectic mornings when you still want something good to eat, try this speedy recipe.

1/2 cup milk
1 egg, well beaten
1/3 cup honey **or** sugar
2 cups Quick Mix (see page 10)

Preheat oven to 400ºF. Combine milk, egg and honey. Add them to Quick Mix. Stir until just blended. Pour batter into a greased and floured 8 x 8 x 2-inch baking pan. Spread with desired topping and bake for 20 minutes, or until done. Makes 1 coffee cake.

BASIC COFFEE CAKE

Surprise! Ten different coffee cakes can be made from this basic recipe! Simply choose your favorite topping from the list on pages 124 and 125.

1/2 cup **each** butter **or** margarine (softened) and honey **or** sugar
1 egg, well beaten
2 cups all purpose flour
1 tbs. baking powder
1/2 tsp. salt
1 tbs. grated lemon **or** orange peel (optional)
1/2 tsp. vanilla (optional)
2/3 cup milk when using honey (3/4 cup milk when using sugar)

Preheat oven to 400°F. Cream butter and honey or sugar. Mix in egg. Stir together flour, baking powder, salt and lemon peel. Add dry ingredients to creamed mixture alternately with the milk and vanilla. Pour batter into a greased and floured 9 x 9 x 2-inch baking pan. Spread desired topping over batter. Bake for 25 to 30 minutes, or until done. Makes 1 coffee cake.

COFFEE CAKE TOPPINGS

Make each topping by first combining the dry ingredients. Then, cut the butter or margarine into the dry ingredients until the mixture is crumbly. Spread over the coffee cake batter and bake as directed.

GRANOLA TOPPING

1 cup granola
1/3 cup brown sugar, firmly packed
1/2 tsp. cinnamon
3 tbs. butter **or** margarine, softened

COCONUT TOPPING

1 cup shredded coconut
1/2 cup chopped pecans **or** walnuts
1/3 cup brown sugar, firmly packed
1/4 cup butter **or** margarine, softened

PECAN WHEAT GERM TOPPING

1/2 cup chopped pecans
1/2 cup wheat germ
1/3 cup brown sugar, firmly packed
1/4 cup butter **or** margarine, softened

124

CINNAMON SUGAR TOPPING

3 tbs. flour (whole wheat **or** unbleached all purpose)
1/3 cup brown sugar, firmly packed
1/2 cup chopped pecans **or** walnuts
1 tsp. cinnamon
1/4 cup butter **or** margarine, softened

APPLE CHEESE TOPPING

Place one cup of peeled, seeded and thinly sliced apples on batter, then add this crumbled mixture:

1/2 cup quick cooking oatmeal
1/2 cup shredded Cheddar cheese
1/3 cup brown sugar, firmly packed
1/4 cup butter **or** margarine, softened

APPLE GRAHAM COFFEE CAKE

Dusted with powdered sugar and served with a generous scoop of vanilla ice cream, this coffee cake becomes a dessert.

1/4 cup butter **or** margarine, softened
1/2 cup brown sugar, firmly packed
1 egg, well beaten
1 cup graham cracker crumbs
1 cup unbleached all purpose flour
2 tsp. baking powder
1/2 tsp. baking soda

1/4 tsp. salt
1/2 tsp. allspice
1 tsp. cinnamon
1/4 cup chopped almonds **or** walnuts
1 cup shredded apple, peeled and cored
1/4 cup milk
powdered sugar (optional)

Preheat oven to 375°F. Cream butter and sugar. Mix in egg. Stir together graham cracker crumbs, flour, baking powder, baking soda, salt, allspice, cinnamon and nuts. Add dry ingredients to creamed mixture alternately with apple and milk. Spread batter into a greased and floured 8 x 8 x 2-inch baking pan. Bake for 35 minutes, or until done. Cool and dust with powdered sugar. Makes 1 coffee cake.

AVOCADO ORANGE COFFEE CAKE

2 cups all purpose flour
3/4 cup brown sugar, firmly packed
1 tbs. baking powder
1/2 tsp. salt   **ORANGE GLAZE:**
1 tsp. cinnamon
1/2 cup chopped pecans **or** walnuts   1/2 cup powdered sugar
3/4 cup mashed avocado   1 tsp. grated orange peel
1/4 cup oil   1 tbs. orange juice
1 egg, well beaten
3/4 cup orange juice

Preheat oven to 400°F. Stir together flour, brown sugar, baking powder, salt, cinnamon and nuts. Mix avocado, oil, egg and orange juice together well. Add this mixture to dry ingredients. Stir until just blended. Spread batter into a greased and floured 9 x 9 x 2-inch baking pan. Bake for 30 minutes, or until done. Combine glaze ingredients. Glaze while warm. Makes 1 coffee cake.

BANANA WHEAT GERM COFFEE CAKE

1/2 cup butter or margarine, softened
2/3 cup honey
2 eggs, well beaten
1-1/4 cups each whole wheat flour and wheat germ
2 tsp. baking powder
1 tsp. baking soda
1/2 tsp. salt
1 cup shredded coconut
1/3 cup buttermilk
1 cup mashed banana

Preheat oven to 350°F. Cream butter and honey. Mix in eggs. Stir together flour, wheat germ, baking powder, baking soda, salt and coconut. Add dry ingredients to creamed mixture alternately with buttermilk and banana. Pour batter into a greased and floured 10-inch tube or bundt pan. Bake for 1 hour, or until done. Cool in pan for 10 minutes, then turn out on wire rack. Sprinkle with powdered sugar. Makes 1 coffee cake.

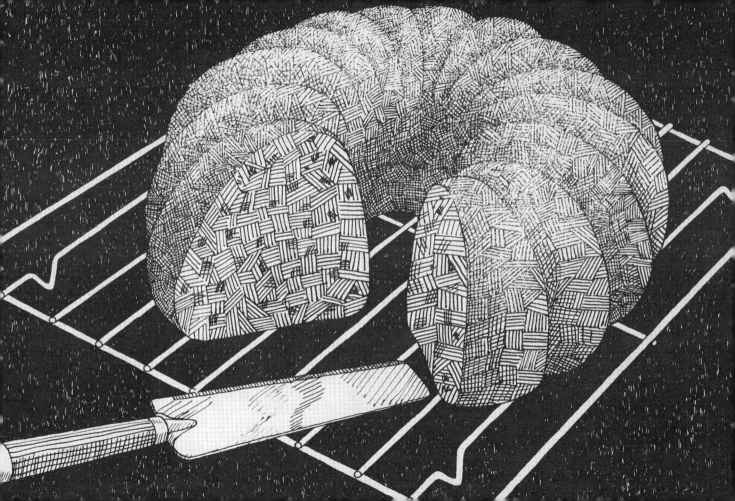

BEER COFFEE CAKE

1 cup butter **or** margarine, softened
1-1/2 cups brown sugar, firmly packed
2 eggs, well beaten
3 cups all purpose flour
2 tsp. baking soda
1/2 tsp. salt
1 tsp. cinnamon
1/2 tsp. **each** allspice and cloves
1 cup chopped walnuts

2 cups chopped dates
12 oz. can beer

LEMON GLAZE:

1 cup powdered sugar
2 tbs. lemon juice
1 tsp. grated lemon peel

Preheat oven to 350°F. Cream butter and sugar. Mix in eggs. Stir together flour, baking soda, salt, cinnamon, allspice, cloves, walnuts and dates. Add the dry ingredients to the creamed mixture alternately with beer. Pour batter into a greased and floured 10-inch tube pan. Bake for 1 hour and 15 minutes, or until done. Cool in pan for about 10 minutes, then turn out on wire rack. Spread on Lemon Glaze. Makes 1 coffee cake.

PINEAPPLE CARROT COFFEE CAKE

1-1/2 cups all purpose flour
3/4 cup brown sugar, firmly packed
2-1/2 tsp. baking powder
1/2 tsp. salt
1 tsp. cinnamon
1 cup shredded carrot
1/2 cup chopped nuts
1/4 cup oil
1 egg, well beaten

8 oz. can crushed pineapple, undrained
1 tsp. vanilla

CREAM CHEESE TOPPING:
3 oz. cream cheese
3 tbs. powdered sugar
1 tbs. milk
1/2 tsp. vanilla

Preheat oven to 350°F. Stir together flour, brown sugar, baking powder, salt, cinnamon, carrots and nuts. Mix the oil, egg, pineapple and vanilla together well. Add this mixture to the dry ingredients. Stir until just blended. Pour batter into a greased and floured 9 x 9 x 2-inch baking pan. Bake for 40 minutes, or until done. Cool, combine topping ingredients until creamy. Spread on coffee cake. Makes 1 coffee cake.

BLUEBERRY BUCKLE COFFEE CAKE

Great-grandma used fresh blueberries for her buckle. If they are not in season use canned or frozen, but be sure to drain, rinse and pat them dry.

1/2 cup butter **or** margarine, softened
1/2 cup sugar
1 egg, well beaten
1 cup whole wheat flour
1 cup unbleached all purpose flour } **or** 2 cups all purpose flour
2-1/2 tsp. baking powder
1/2 tsp. baking soda
1/2 tsp. salt
2/3 cup buttermilk
2 cups blueberries
Topping (see next page)

Preheat oven to 375°F. Cream butter and sugar. Mix in egg. Stir together flour, baking powder, baking soda and salt. Add the dry ingredients to creamed mixture alternately with buttermilk. Gently, stir in blueberries. Spread batter in a greased and floured 9 x 9 x 2-inch baking pan. Bake for 50 minutes, or until done. Serve warm. Makes 1 coffee cake.

TOPPING

1/2 cup sugar
1/3 cup flour (whole wheat **or** all purpose)
1/2 tsp. cinnamon
1/4 cup butter **or** margarine, softened

Combine sugar, flour and cinnamon. Cut butter into dry ingredients until mixture is crumbly.

CHUCK'S CHOCOLATE CHIP COFFEE CAKE

1/2 cup butter **or** margarine, softened
3/4 cup sugar
2 eggs, well beaten
2 cups unbleached all purpose flour   **TOPPING:**
1 tbs. baking powder
1/2 tsp. salt   1/2 cup chopped pecans **or** walnuts
1 cup milk   1 tbs. sugar
1 tsp. vanilla
1 cup mini chocolate chips

Preheat oven to 350°F. Cream butter and sugar. Mix in eggs. Stir together flour, baking powder and salt. Add dry ingredients to creamed mixture alternately with milk and vanilla. Stir in chocolate chips. Spread batter into a greased and floured 9 x 9 x 2-inch baking pan. Combine topping ingredients. Sprinkle on topping and bake for 40 minutes, or until done. Makes 1 coffee cake.

PEANUT BUTTER COFFEE CAKE

3/4 cup milk
1 egg, well beaten
1/2 cup honey

1/4 cup peanut butter
2-1/2 cups Quick Mix (see page 10)
Topping (see below)

Preheat oven to 400°F. Mix milk, egg, honey and peanut butter together well. Add liquid ingredients to the Quick Mix. Stir until just blended. Spread in a greased and floured 9 x 9 x 2-inch baking pan. Spread with Topping and bake for 20 to 25 minutes, or until done. Serve warm. Makes 1 coffee cake.

TOPPING

1/2 cup Quick Mix (see page 10)
1/2 cup brown sugar, firmly packed
1/4 cup **each** chopped unsalted peanuts and butter **or** margarine

Stir together Quick Mix, brown sugar and peanuts. Cut butter into the dry ingredients until the mixture is crumbly. Sprinkle over the batter.

OATMEAL COCONUT COFFEE CAKE

A lunchbox treat for children.

1 cup quick-cooking oatmeal
1/2 cup butter **or** margarine, cut into 5 slices
1-1/3 cup boiling water
3/4 cup sugar
3/4 cup brown sugar, firmly packed
2 eggs, well beaten
3/4 cup whole wheat flour
3/4 cup unbleached all purpose flour } **or** 1-1/2 cups all purpose flour
2 tsp. baking powder
1 tsp. baking soda
1/4 tsp. salt
1 tsp. cinnamon
1/2 tsp. nutmeg
Coconut Topping (see page 137)

Preheat oven to 350°F. Combine oatmeal, butter and boiling water. Let stand for 20 minutes. Beat together sugars and eggs. Stir together flour, baking powder, baking soda, salt, cinnamon and nutmeg. Add dry ingredients to sugar and eggs alternately with oatmeal mixture. Pour batter into a greased and floured 9 x 13-inch baking pan. Bake for 35 minutes, or until done. Spread with topping and broil until the topping is golden brown. Serve warm. Makes 1 coffee cake.

COCONUT TOPPING

1/3 cup butter **or** margarine, melted
3/4 cup brown sugar, firmly packed
1/4 cup milk
1 cup coconut
1 cup chopped nuts

Combine ingredients.

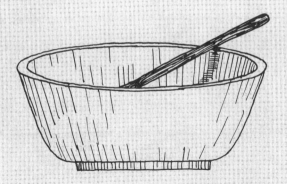

PRUNE COFFEE CAKE

1/2 cup butter **or** margarine, softened
1-1/2 cups sugar
3 eggs, well beaten
2 tsp. vanilla
2-1/2 cups all purpose flour
2 tsp. baking powder
1 tsp. baking soda
1/2 tsp. salt

1 tsp. cinnamon
1 tsp. allspice
1/2 tsp. cloves
1 cup buttermilk
1 cup chopped pecans **or** walnuts
1 cup chopped dried prunes
powdered sugar (optional)

Preheat oven to 350°F. Cream butter and sugar. Mix in eggs and vanilla. Stir together flour, baking powder, baking soda, salt, cinnamon, allspice and cloves. Add dry ingredients to creamed mixture alternately with buttermilk. Stir in nuts and prunes. Pour batter into a greased and floured 10-inch tube or bundt pan. Bake for 65 minutes or until done. Cool in pan for 5 minutes, then turn out on wire rack. Dust with powdered sugar. Makes 1 coffee cake.

UPSIDE DOWN COFFEE CAKE

Don't limit yourself to just pineapple for this upside down cake. Try apples or bananas instead! See page 142 for the variations.

1/2 cup butter **or** margarine, softened
1/2 cup sugar
1 egg, well beaten
1 cup whole wheat flour
1 cup unbleached all purpose flour } **or** 2 cups all purpose flour
1 tbs. baking powder
1/2 tsp. salt
2/3 cup milk
3 tbs. butter **or** margarine
1/4 cup brown sugar, firmly packed
1 of the variations (see page 142)

Preheat oven to 375°F. Cream butter and sugar. Mix in egg. Stir together flour, baking powder and salt. Add dry ingredients to creamed mixture alternately with milk. Set aside. Melt 3 tablespoons of butter in a 9 x 9 x 2-inch baking pan in oven. Sprinkle brown sugar over butter. Arrange fruit, cut side up, in an attractive pattern, in the pan, **or** sprinkle on coconut and pecans. Spread batter into pan and bake for 30 to 35 minutes. Remove from oven and immediately invert pan, keeping pan on the cake for several minutes. Remove pan and serve warm. Makes 1 coffee cake.

VARIATIONS FOR UPSIDE DOWN COFFEE CAKE

- 9 pineapple rings with a maraschino cherry in the center of each.
- 2 cups of peeled and cored apple slices, 1/4 cup raisins, 1/4 cup walnut halves and 1/2 teaspoon of cinnamon.
- 1 cup of banana slices. Brush the cake with 3 tablespoons of rum before serving.
- 1 cup of fruit cocktail or sliced canned fruit, drained well. Brush the cake with 3 tablespoons of brandy before serving.
- 1/2 cup of coconut and 1/2 cup of pecans.

HEALTH COFFEE CAKE

1/2 cup soy flour
1 cup all purpose flour
1/3 cup wheat germ
2 tbs. bran flakes
1/3 cup powdered milk
1 tbs. baking powder
1 tsp. baking soda
1/4 tsp. salt
1/2 cup **each** chopped dates **or** raisins and chopped nuts
1 cup yogurt
1 egg, well beaten
1/4 cup oil
1 tbs. molasses
3 tbs. honey
2 tbs. orange juice
Topping (see next page)

Preheat oven to 350°F. Stir together flours, wheat germ, bran, powdered milk, baking powder, baking soda, salt, dates and nuts. Mix yogurt, egg, oil, molasses, honey and orange juice together well. Add this mixture to dry ingredients. Stir until just blended. Pour batter into a greased and floured 9 x 9 x 2-inch baking pan. Sprinkle on topping. Bake for 35 minutes, or until done. Makes 1 coffee cake.

TOPPING

1/4 cup wheat germ
1/3 cup date sugar, **or** brown sugar, firmly packed
1/4 cup chopped pecans **or** walnuts
1 tsp. cinnamon
1/4 cup butter **or** margarine, softened

Stir together wheat germ, date sugar, nuts and cinnamon. Cut butter into the dry ingredients until mixture is crumbly.

PUMPKIN COFFEE CAKE

2 cups Quick Mix (see page 10)
1/2 cup brown sugar, firmly packed
1/2 tsp. cinnamon
1/4 tsp. **each** ginger and cloves
1/2 cup raisins
1/2 cup chopped nuts
1/4 cup milk
2 eggs, well beaten
3/4 cup canned pumpkin

TOPPING:

2 tbs. Quick Mix
1/4 cup brown sugar, firmly packed
1/2 tsp. cinnamon
2 tbs. chopped pecans **or** walnuts
2 tbs. butter **or** margarine

Preheat oven to 350°F. Stir together Quick Mix, brown sugar, cinnamon, ginger, cloves, raisins and nuts. Mix milk, eggs and pumpkin together well. Add liquid ingredients to dry ingredients. Stir until just blended. Spread batter in a greased and floured 8 x 8 x 2-inch baking pan. Prepare topping. Combine dry ingredients. Cut in butter until mixture is crumbly. Sprinkle on topping and bake for 40 minutes, or until done. Serve warm. Makes 1 coffee cake.

BERTHA'S COFFEE CAKE

1-1/2 cups unbleached all purpose flour
1/2 cup brown sugar, firmly packed
1/3 cup sugar
1 tsp. cinnamon
1/2 tsp. **each** nutmeg and ginger
1/2 cup oil

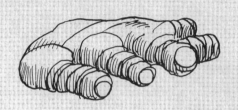

Preheat oven to 350°F. Stir together flour, sugars and spices. Blend in oil. Set aside 1/2 cup of this mixture. To the remainder add:

2 tsp. baking powder   1 egg, well beaten
1/2 tsp. baking soda   1/2 cup sour cream
1/2 tsp. salt

Mix well and spread in a greased and floured 8 x 8 x 2-inch baking pan. Sprinkle 1/2 cup of the reserved mixture on the batter. Bake for 30 minutes, or until done. Makes 1 coffee cake.

PANCAKES, WAFFLES AND POPOVERS

Who can resist the wonderful aroma of fresh baked pancakes or waffles in the morning? Top these breakfast favorites with honey butter or spicy applesauce (see page 176). For a quick dinner that is sure to please, add sherried crab sauce to pancakes or waffles.

Follow these suggestions for the best results possible:

• For pancakes and waffles, stir together the liquid and dry ingredients only until they are just moistened. Do not overmix. The batter will be slightly lumpy.

• For lighter pancakes or waffles, separate the egg and beat the white until stiff, but not dry. Fold it into the batter.

• Cook pancakes at 380°F., unless otherwise directed.

• It is only necessary to lightly oil the surface of the pan for the first batch of pancakes.

• Pancakes are cooked most easily and with the best results on an electric griddle or in an electric frying pan.

• Pancakes are done when bubbles appear, and the edges of the "cake" are dry. You may also wish to check the underside of the pancake to see if it is browned. Merely pick up an edge of the "cake" with a spatula and take a peek. Remember, the second side of the pancake takes less time to cook.

• For waffles, preheat the waffle iron to the hottest temperature possible. When a drop of water sizzles on the surface, you may add the batter.

• Spoon or pour the waffle batter onto the preheated iron to about 1 inch from the edge. This will allow the waffle to expand and rise without spilling over the edges of your iron.

• Waffles are done when they have stopped steaming, or when they have reached the desired degree of brownness. The longer you bake the waffle, the more crisp it will be.

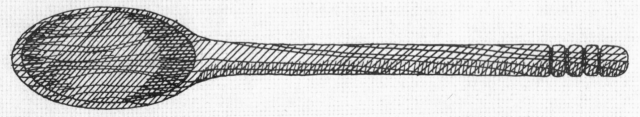

QUICK STACK

Rushing in the morning? Make our Quick Pancakes!

2 cups Quick Mix (see page 10)
1 tbs. sugar or honey
1 egg, well beaten
1-1/4 cups milk

Stir together Quick Mix and sugar. Mix egg and milk together well. Add this mixture to dry ingredients. Stir only until moistened. If thinner pancakes are desired, add more milk. Pour or spoon batter onto a hot griddle or frying pan. Cook until golden brown. Makes about 8 medium-sized pancakes. Serve hot with butter, syrup, honey or jam.

BASIC PANCAKES

Try a stack of hot pancakes, topped with our syrups. Watch your family's eyes light up!

3/4 cup whole wheat flour
3/4 cup unbleached all purpose flour } **or** 1-1/2 cups all purpose flour
2-1/2 tsp. baking powder
1/2 tsp. salt
1 tbs. sugar **or** honey
1 egg, well beaten
1-1/4 cups milk
3 tbs. melted butter, margarine **or** oil

Stir together flour, baking powder, salt and sugar. Mix egg, milk and butter together well. Add this mixture to dry ingredients. Stir only until moistened. If thinner pancakes are desired, add more milk. Pour or spoon batter onto a hot griddle or frying pan. Cook until golden brown. Makes about 10 medium-sized pancakes. Serve hot with butter, syrup, honey or jam.

150

PANCAKE VARIATIONS

Add any one of the following ingredients to the pancake batter.

- 1/2 cup chopped dates
- 3/4 cup blueberries, rinsed and patted dry if canned or frozen
- 1/3 cup fried bacon, crumbled
- 1/2 cup chopped pecans **or** walnuts
- Replace milk with buttermilk and add 1/2 teaspoon of baking soda.
- Substitute 1/2 cup quick-cooking oatmeal for 1/2 cup of flour.
- **Grandpa Jack's Peach Pancakes** Replace 1/4 cup of milk with 1/4 cup of canned peach juice and add 1/2 cup chopped canned peaches.
- Spoon 2 tablespoons of fresh fruit on a pancake, roll it up and dust with powdered sugar.
- Pour the batter into various sizes and shapes, such as a snowman, a mouse, a butterfly or your child's initials.

AL'S BUCKWHEAT PANCAKES

My husband's favorite flapjacks.

1-1/2 cups whole wheat flour
1/2 cup buckwheat flour
1 tbs. baking powder
1/2 tsp. salt
2 cups milk
1/2 cup oil
2 tbs. molasses (optional)
3 eggs, separated

Stir together wheat flour, buckwheat flour, baking powder and salt. Mix milk, oil, molasses and egg yolks together well. Add this mixture to dry ingredients. Stir only until moistened. Beat egg whites until stiff, and fold them into batter. Pour or spoon batter onto a hot griddle or frying pan. Cook until golden brown. Makes about 16 medium-sized pancakes.

BOB'S BUTTERMILK PANCAKES

Add blueberries to this recipe and come up with everybody's favorite—blueberry pancakes!

2 cups all purpose flour
1 tsp. baking soda
1/2 tsp. salt
2 cups buttermilk
3 eggs, separated
1/4 cup melted butter or margarine
1 cup blueberries (optional, rinsed well and patted dry if they are canned or frozen)

Stir together flour, baking soda and salt. Combine buttermilk, egg yolks and melted butter. Add this mixture to dry ingredients. Stir until just moistened. Beat egg whites until stiff, and fold them into batter. Gently fold in blueberries, if desired. Pour or spoon batter onto a hot griddle or frying pan. Cook until golden brown. Makes about 18 medium-sized pancakes.

SOUR CREAM PANCAKES

1 cup whole wheat flour
1/2 cup wheat germ
2 tbs. bran flakes
1-1/2 tsp. baking powder
1/4 tsp. baking soda
1/2 tsp. salt
1/2 cup sour cream
1 egg, separated
2 tbs. honey **or** molasses
1-1/4 cups milk
3 tbs. melted butter, margarine **or** oil

    Stir together flour, wheat germ, bran, baking powder, baking soda and salt. Mix sour cream, egg yolk, honey, milk and butter together well. Add this mixture to the dry ingredients. Stir until just moistened. Beat egg white until stiff and fold it into batter. Pour or spoon batter onto a hot griddle or frying pan. Cook until golden brown. Makes 10 to 12 medium-sized pancakes.

HEALTH PANCAKES

When the kids clamor for pancakes and you are thinking "nutrition," this hotcake is the perfect solution.

1/2 cup soy flour
1/2 cup whole wheat flour
1/2 cup unbleached all purpose flour } **or** 1 cup all purpose flour
2 tbs. **each** wheat germ, bran flakes and powdered milk
1 tbs. baking powder
1/2 tsp. baking soda
1/4 tsp. salt
2 tsp. grated orange peel
1/2 cup yogurt
2 eggs, separated
3 tbs. oil
1 tbs. molasses **or** honey
1 cup orange juice

Stir together flours, wheat germ, bran, powdered milk, baking powder, baking soda, salt and orange peel. Mix yogurt, egg yolks, oil, molasses and orange juice together well. Add this mixture to the dry ingredients. Stir until just moistened. Beat egg whites until stiff and fold them into batter. Pour or spoon batter onto a moderately hot (350°F.) griddle or frying pan. (Soy flour browns quickly.) Cook until golden brown. Makes 10 to 12 pancakes.

CREPES

The popularity of crepes has grown tremendously over the last few years. Serve these delicious thin "pancakes" for breakfast, lunch, dinner or dessert.

1/2 cup milk
1/2 cup water
2 eggs
1 cup unbleached all purpose flour
1/2 tsp. salt
oil (a few drops for each crepe)

Combine all ingredients in a blender, and agitate until smooth. Refrigerate batter for two hours or overnight. Heat crepe pan or small frying pan to a fairly high temperature. Brush pan with oil. Pour about 2 tablespoons of batter into pan. Tilt quickly to coat pan with batter. Pour off excess batter. When browned on the bottom, turn. Cook until brown and stack on a plate. Repeat process using the remaining batter. Grease pan between crepes. Makes about 14 crepes. To serve, fill each crepe with one of our dinner or dessert sauces (see pages 175 through 179).

For dessert crepes, add all of the following ingredients to the above batter.

1 tsp. brandy
1/2 tsp. grated orange **or** lemon peel
1 tbs. sugar

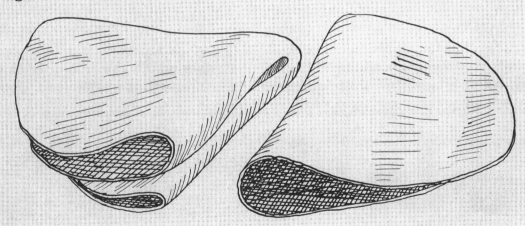

QUICK WAFFLES

Be creative with any one of our numerous waffle variations on page 162.

2 cups Quick Mix (see page 10)
2 tbs. honey **or** sugar
2 eggs, separated
1 cup milk

Stir together Quick Mix and honey. Mix egg yolks and milk together well. Add this mixture to dry ingredients. Stir until just blended. Beat egg whites until stiff and fold them into batter. Pour or spoon batter onto a hot waffle iron. Cook waffles to desired doneness. Makes 4 to 6 waffles.

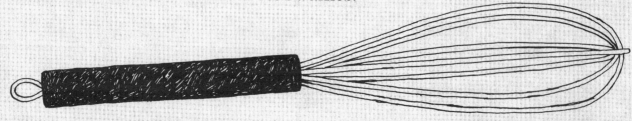

BASIC WAFFLES

When you are baking waffles, double the recipe and freeze the leftovers. Just pop them into the toaster when you have the urge for a waffle, but not the time to mix up a fresh batch.

1 cup whole wheat flour
1 cup unbleached all purpose flour } **or** 2 cups all purpose flour
1 tbs. baking powder
1/2 tsp. salt
2 tbs. sugar
2 eggs, separated
6 tbs. melted butter, margarine **or** oil
1-1/2 cups milk

Stir together flour, baking powder, salt and sugar. Mix egg yolks, butter and milk together well. Add this mixture to dry ingredients. Stir until just blended. Beat egg whites until stiff and fold them into batter. Pour or spoon batter onto a hot waffle iron. Cook waffles to desired doneness. Makes 5 to 7 waffles.

WAFFLE VARIATIONS

Add any one of the following ingredients to the waffle batter.

- 2/3 cup diced banana and 1/4 cup bran flakes
- 1/2 cup grated apple and 1/2 teaspoon cinnamon
- 1/2 cup chopped dates and 1/4 cup chopped nuts
- 3/4 cup blueberries (rinsed and patted dry if they are canned or frozen)
- 1/3 cup coconut and 1/3 cup chopped nuts
- 1/2 cup chopped pecans or walnuts
- 1/3 cup shredded cheddar cheese and 1/4 cup fried bacon, crumbled
- Replace the milk with buttermilk and add 1/2 teaspoon of baking soda.
- Reduce the butter, margarine or oil to 1/4 cup and add 1/3 cup of chunky peanut butter to the liquid ingredients.
- Replace 3/4 cup milk with 3/4 cup orange juice and add 1 tablespoon of grated orange peel.

162

CORN WAFFLES

A great dinner waffle topped with our chili (see page 179).

1-1/2 cups all purpose flour
1/2 cup yellow cornmeal
1 tbs. baking powder
1/2 tsp. salt
2 tbs. sugar
1 cup canned whole kernal corn, drained
2 eggs, separated
6 tbs. melted butter, margarine **or** oil
1-1/2 cups milk

Stir together flour, cornmeal, baking powder, salt and sugar. Mix corn, egg yolks, butter and milk together well. Add this mixture to dry ingredients. Stir until just blended. Beat egg whites until stiff and fold them into batter. Pour or spoon batter onto a hot waffle iron. Cook waffles to desired doneness. Makes 5 to 7 waffles.

GINGERBREAD WAFFLES

Serve these waffles with our warm spicy applesauce (see page 176).

2 cups all purpose flour
1 tbs. baking powder
1/2 tsp. salt
1/2 tsp. cinnamon
1/4 tsp. **each** ginger and nutmeg

2 tbs. sugar
1/2 cup molasses
2 eggs, separated
6 tbs. melted butter, margarine **or** oil
1 cup milk

Stir together flour, baking powder, salt, cinnamon, ginger, nutmeg and sugar. Mix molasses, egg yolks, butter and milk together well. Add this mixture to dry ingredients. Stir until just blended. Beat egg whites until stiff and fold them into batter. Pour or spoon batter onto a hot waffle iron. Cook waffles to desired doneness. Makes 5 to 7 waffles.

HEALTH WAFFLES

1/2 cup soy flour
1 cup all purpose flour
2 tbs. wheat germ
1/3 cup bran flakes
2 tbs. powdered milk
1 tbs. baking powder
1/2 tsp. baking soda

1/4 tsp. salt
1/2 cup yogurt
2 eggs, separated
1/3 cup oil
1 tbs. molasses
1 cup orange juice

Stir together flours, wheat germ, bran flakes, powdered milk, baking powder, baking soda and salt. Mix yogurt, egg yolks, oil, molasses and orange juice together well. Add this mixture to the dry ingredients. Stir until just blended. Beat egg whites until stiff and fold them into batter. Pour or spoon batter onto a hot waffle iron. Cook waffles to desired doneness. Makes 5 to 7 waffles.

SOUR CREAM WALNUT WAFFLES

1 cup whole wheat flour
1 cup unbleached all purpose flour } **or** 2 cups all purpose flour
2-1/2 tsp. baking powder
1/2 tsp. **each** baking soda and salt
2/3 cup chopped walnuts
2 tbs. sugar
2 eggs, separated
6 tbs. melted butter, margarine **or** oil
1-1/2 cups milk
3/4 cup sour cream

Stir together flour, baking powder, baking soda, salt, nuts and sugar. Mix egg yolks, butter, milk and sour cream together well. Add this mixture to dry ingredients. Stir until just blended. Beat egg whites until stiff and fold them into batter. Pour or spoon batter onto a hot waffle iron. Cook waffles to desired doneness. Makes 6 to 8 waffles.

CHRISTINE'S DANISH AEBLESKIVERS

Katherine's Great Grandmother brought this recipe and her aebleskiver pan to California from Denmark in the 1890's. The pan was handed down from mother to daughter for generations. Katherine is still using it! An aebleskiver pan is about 8 inches in diameter. It is basically a skillet with 8 indentations in which the aebleskiver batter cooks.

3/4 cup whole wheat flour
3/4 cup unbleached all purpose flour } **or** 1-1/2 cups all purpose flour
2 tsp. baking powder
1/2 tsp. salt
1 tbs. sugar
2 eggs, separated
1 cup milk
oil
aebleskiver pan
2 bananas **or** 1 small can of peaches, well drained (optional)
powdered sugar

168

Stir together flour, baking powder, salt and sugar. Mix egg yolks and milk together well. Add this mixture to the dry ingredients. Stir until just blended. Beat egg whites until stiff and fold them into batter. Heat aebleskiver pan. Spoon 1/2 teaspoon oil into each section and fill 2/3 full with batter. Cook over medium heat until bubbles appear. Turn with a fork or skewer and cook the other side until lightly browned. To vary flavor, add a slice of banana or peach to each section before it is turned. Dust with powdered sugar and serve with butter and jam or syrup. Makes about 28 aebleskivers.

SYRUPS, SPREADS AND SAUCES

This section will enable you to be even more creative with our quick bread recipes.

Make your own warm "maple" syrup and really do our pancakes and waffles justice. The next time you bake a loaf for a gift, include a little pot of one of our sweet or savory spreads. It will make your gift doubly delicious. Turn one of the biscuits, waffle or crepe recipes into an exciting and out-of-the-ordinary dinner treat by adding one of our sauces. How do sherried crab waffles or Crepes Ratatouilles sound?

HOMEMADE "MAPLE" SYRUP

1 cup brown sugar, firmly packed
2/3 cup water

2 tbs. butter or margarine
1/2 tsp. maple or vanilla flavoring

Boil brown sugar and water in a saucepan for 5 minutes. Stir in butter or margarine and flavoring. Serve warm.

VARIATIONS FOR "MAPLE" SYRUP

Add any one of the following ingredients to one cup homemade "maple" syrup or commercial maple syrup. Heat in a saucepan and serve warm.

- 2 tsp. grated orange peel
- 1/4 cup chopped pecans and 2 tbs. butter or margarine
- 1/4 cup light cream
- 2 tbs. sherry, 2 tbs. butter or margarine, and dash of cinnamon and nutmeg

HONEY BUTTER SYRUP

Instead of pouring cold honey on your pancakes or waffles, why not try this warm syrup.

1 cup honey
1/4 cup butter

Heat in saucepan on medium heat until the butter melts. Serve warm.

VARIATIONS

Add any one of the following ingredients to the Honey Butter Syrup.

- 1/4 tsp. cinnamon and 1/4 tsp. nutmeg
- 2 tsp. grated orange peel
- 1/4 cup shredded coconut and 1/4 cup light cream **or** milk

BUTTER SPREADS

To make your quick breads extra special, try a sweet or savory butter spread on top.

SWEET AND SAVORY BUTTERS

Add one of the following suggestions to 1/2 cup of soft butter. If desired, whip the butter in the mixer until fluffy.

- 1/4 cup honey **or** maple syrup
- 2 tsp. grated lemon **or** orange peel and 1 tbs. powdered sugar **or** honey.
- 1 peach, peeled and chopped, 1 tsp. lemon juice, 2 tbs. brown sugar **or** honey, dash cinnamon.
- 1-1/2 cups powdered sugar, 1/2 tsp. vanilla, and 2 tbs. brandy, bourbon **or** rum.
- 1 tbs. snipped parsley, 1/4 tsp. oregano, 1/4 tsp. dill and 1 clove minced garlic
- 2 tbs. snipped chives **or** parsley
- 3 tbs. Parmesan cheese, 1/4 tsp. marjoram and 1/4 tsp. basil.

SWEET CREAM CHEESE SPREADS

Add protein to your quick breads with a cream cheese spread.

Add one of the following to 8 ounces of softened cream cheese:

- 2 tsp. grated orange peel and 2 tbs. honey **or** sugar
- 3 tbs. orange marmalade
- 1/4 cup chopped dates **or** raisins
- 1/4 cup chopped nuts
- 3 tbs. maple syrup

TROPICAL FRUIT SPREAD

1 tbs. honey **or** sugar
1/3 cup crushed pineapple, drained
1 tsp. grated orange peel

1/4 cup shredded coconut
8 oz. pkg. cream cheese, softened

Mix the ingredients until blended.

BRANDIED FRUIT SAUCE

Serve with shortcake, pancakes, crepes or waffles.

21 oz. can cherry **or** blueberry pie filling
1 tsp. grated lemon peel
3 tbs. brandy
2 tbs. butter **or** margarine

Heat the above ingredients in a small saucepan until warm.

SPICY APPLESAUCE

Serve warm over pancakes or waffles.

1 lb. can applesauce   1/4 tsp. cinnamon
1 tbs. butter **or** margarine   1/4 tsp. nutmeg

Heat the above ingredients in a small saucepan until warm.

176

RATATOUILLE

A bountiful harvest of vegetables to serve with herb biscuits or muffins.

2 tbs. oil
1 large white onion, sliced
1 clove garlic, crushed
1 small eggplant, peeled and cubed
3 medium zucchini, thickly sliced
1/4 lb. fresh mushrooms, halved
3 carrots, peeled and sliced
1 small green pepper, cut in strips
2 large tomatoes, skinned and chunked
2 tbs. snipped parsley
1 tsp. **each** salt and basil

Saute onion and garlic in oil until tender. Add remaining ingredients and simmer covered for about 30 minutes, or until vegetables are done. Makes 5 to 6 servings.

SHERRIED CRAB SAUCE

A San Francisco favorite! Great over waffles.

2 tbs. butter **or** margarine
2 tsp. flour (whole wheat **or** all purpose)
1 cup light cream **or** milk
1 cup crab meat **or** 7-1/2 oz. can crab, drained and flaked
salt and pepper to taste
dash nutmeg
3 tbs. dry sherry

Melt butter in saucepan. Stir in flour. Gradually add cream. Stir until thickened. Add remaining ingredients and heat until warm. Makes 6 servings.

CHILI

For a South-of-the-Border treat, serve piping hot chili over cornbread.

1 tbs. oil
1 cup chopped onion
1 clove garlic, crushed
1 lb. ground beef
16 oz. can tomatoes, undrained
4 oz. can chopped green chilies
1 tsp. salt

1 tbs. chili powder (or more to taste)
1 tsp. ground cumin
1 bay leaf
1/2 tsp. oregano
1 whole small red pepper
16 oz. can red kidney beans, drained

In frying pan, saute onion and garlic in oil until tender. Add ground beef and brown. Drain fat. Stir in tomatoes, chilies, salt, chili powder, cumin, bay leaf, oregano and red pepper. Simmer covered for about two hours, stirring occasionally. Add a little water if chili is too thick. Add beans and heat until warm. Remove bay leaf and red pepper before serving. Makes 4 to 6 servings.

INDEX

PANCAKES AND WAFFLES

SYRUPS, SPREADS AND SAUCES